English Castles

22

English Castles

R. ALLEN BROWN

B. T. BATSFORD LTD LONDON

First published 1954
First paperback edition 1962

*For copyright reasons, this book may not be
issued to the public on loan or otherwise except
in its original soft cover.*

Revised Edition © R. Allen Brown, 1962

PRINTED AND BOUND IN DENMARK BY
F. E. BORDING LTD, COPENHAGEN AND LONDON
FOR THE PUBLISHERS
B. T. BATSFORD LTD
4 FITZHARDINGE STREET, PORTMAN SQUARE, LONDON W. I

Preface

THOUGH this book makes no claim to be a work of original scholarship, it does, at least in part, attempt something new. In the last half-century there have been several good books upon the English castle, but all of them have been concerned with its architectural history only, and generally speaking this is also true of the very many articles upon individual castles to be found in local histories and the publications of local antiquarian societies. The history of the English castle in the full and proper sense has never yet been written. Nor, of course, will it be found in the pages which follow, but merely a tentative reconnaissance towards the ideal.

After an introductory chapter concerned with the definition and origin of the castle, the next four chapters of this book are devoted to medieval military architecture. Here, then, there is little new, and I freely acknowledge my debt in particular to E. S. Armitage, *Early Norman Castles of the British Isles,* and A. Hamilton Thompson, *Military Architecture in England during the Middle Ages,* and also to the more recent works of Mr. Sidney Toy and Dr. W. Douglas Simpson. In this section of the book the attempt has been simply to provide a clear and concise account of the architectural development and decline of the English castle. Within this account two points in particular have been stressed. First, the twin basic facts, that the castle was introduced into this country by the Normans in the eleventh century, and was then almost invariably not a fortress of stone but a stronghold of earthwork and timber, have been strongly emphasised; for though well established now for the last fifty years, they are still anything but common knowledge. No one, I suppose, would mistake a church of whatever period for anything but a church, yet there are many who never recognise in the mounds and earthworks which they see, or could see, the authentic survivals of early Norman castles, and the conviction that a castle can only be a building or ruin of stone remains the most deep-rooted of misconceptions. The second point which it seemed necessary to emphasise is the essential continuity of English medieval military architecture. Only very rarely can we point to a castle as a complete example of the fortification of this or that period. The architectural history of the vast majority of our castles is one of continuous development from an early origin, so that the typical castle shows work of almost every generation from the eleventh to the sixteenth century.

But the castle is much more than an Ancient Monument divorced from reality, and its history comprises much more than mere architectural description and explanation. We may first enquire how such impressive monuments were built, and wonder also a little how much they cost. Even more important are the two fundamental questions of *what* was a castle and *why* was a castle. And in asking why castles were built, what were their uses and wherein lay their importance, we shall be led on to enquire also how many castles there were in the medieval English kingdom and where they were situated. To give some answer to these questions is the object of the second half of this book, while, finally, the attempt to define and explain the importance of the castle in medieval life and society demands some explanation of why that importance came eventually to decline.

The geographical purview of this book is confined to England and Wales, for Scotland, by virtue of its medieval independence, remains a separate story. For the rest, the castle is placed firmly in the Middle Ages where it belongs, and for this there can be no apology. In the later chapters, however, dealing with history as opposed to architecture, there may also be observed a certain bias towards the earlier Middle Ages of the twelfth and thirteenth centuries. In part this bias results from personal preference, and may perhaps be thus excused, since a man should surely write about what he most enjoys. Yet its main defence is that the study of castles from every point of view save the architectural has been much neglected, and previous work along the lines attempted in these chapters has been directed upon the earlier period. The resulting paucity of information for the later Middle Ages is to some extent made less serious by the fact that the castle was at the height of its importance in England and Wales precisely in those twelfth and thirteenth centuries upon which our attentions are of necessity concentrated.

To name all those who have helped directly or indirectly in the making of this book is impossible if the Preface to it is to be kept within reasonable bounds. Amongst the latter, however, I must not omit to express my obligation to Mr. J. O. Prestwich of The Queen's College, Oxford, who first introduced me to the study of English castles. Amongst the former I must break with precedent in naming first my wife, who encouraged me throughout the venture, typed the manuscript, drew some of the illustrations and helped with the index. To Mr. Gilbert Howes I am greatly indebted for many of the plans and line drawings, and the map. I must also thank Mr. A. D. M. Cox of University College, Oxford, for carefully reading the manuscript and offering valuable criticism, gratefully incorporated; and Mr. G. B. Audley who performer a similar office even while much occupied with more important matters. To the Publishers I am extremely grateful for giving me the opportunity to write the book, and for their friendly help, no less than skill, in every phase of its preparation. Finally, since the text carries no system of footnotes, I can only express a general obligation to all those whose work I have read and used in writing it.

Yet, in spite of all and so much help, I must alone take the responsibility for the errors that will inevitably be discovered in the following pages. The history of English medieval castles is a large subject, largely neglected, and terrifyingly requiring, of one rash enough to attempt it, a knowledge of the whole Middle Ages by no means acquired.

'Dauntless the slug-horn to my lips I set,
And blew, "*Childe Roland to the Dark Tower came*".'

Walberswick, Suffolk   R. A. B.

Note to the Second Edition

THE opportunity for revision afforded by the issue of this book in paperback form has been gladly accepted. The text, however, stands much as it was, and the alterations are confined to matters of detail together with the replacement of some of the plans by others more up to date (the plan of Caerphilly remains less than satisfactory because nothing better was available). Almost all these corrections result from research carried out by many scholars in the last few years, and I am grateful especially to Mr. H. M. Colvin, Mr. A. J. Taylor and Mr. A. R. Duftie for allowing me to profit from their very considerable contribution to it. Like all students of English history and architecture I am perhaps most indebted to the Ministry of Works and the Royal Commission on Historic Monuments, without whose labours of preserving and recording studies of this kind could scarcely be undertaken. *Si monumentum* ... etc. etc.

Kew, January 1962   R. A. B.

Contents

Acknowledgment

THE Author and Publishers wish to thank the following for permission to reproduce the photographic illustrations in this book: Aerofilms and Aero Pictorial Ltd. for figs. 1, 2, 7, 8, 14, 20, 21, 25–27, 36, 37, 43 and 47; Airviews Ltd. for fig. 24; Hallam Ashley, F. R. P. S. for figs. 11 and 30; Donovan E. H. Box for fig. 45; J. Allan Cash, F. R. P. S. for fig. 16; the Governing Body of Christ Church, Oxford for fig. 41; the Master and Fellows of Corpus Christi, Cambridge for fig. 42; Country Life Ltd. for fig. 17; the Warden of the Durham Colleges for fig. 44; T. Edmondson for figs. 9 and 48; Leonard and Marjorie Gayton for figs. 28, 32, 33 and 35; F. A. Girling for fig. 6; A. F. Kersting, F. R. P. S. for figs. 10, 13, 15, 29, 31 and 34; the Ministry of Works (Crown Copyright Reserved) for fig. 18; the Mustograph Agency for fig. 12; National Buildings Record for fig. 40; Paul Popper Ltd. for figs. 22 and 23; the Deputy Keeper of the Public Records for figs. 38, 39 and 46; Roger Schall, Paris for fig. 19; Raphael Tuck and Sons Ltd. for fig. 49.

Acknowledgment is also due to the Trustees of the British Museum for permission to reproduce the diagrams on pages 141, 143, 144, and 149, from the fourteenth-century *De Re Militari* of Robert Valturius; to the Controller of H. M. Stationery Office for the plans on pages 63, 75, 77, 82, 83, from the Ministry of Works guide-books to the castles of Flint, Carnarvon, Conway, Rhuddlan, Caerphilly and Raglan; and to the Royal Commission on Historical Monuments for the plans on pages 46–7, 48 and 78, from their publications *Essex, Westmorland and Anglesey*, and also for supplying the information upon which the plan on page 86 is based. That on page 64 is based on material provided by Archives Photographiques des Monuments Historiques, Paris.

The plans on pages 49 and 53 are after drawings by G. T. Clark, and those on pages 52, 81 and 96 after H. Munro Cautley, C. R. Peers and A. W. Chapham respectively. The plan on page 99 is from Lord Curzon's *Bodiam Castle*.

List of Illustrations

THE PLATES

Page

Map of the castles
mentioned in the text

Statute Miles

G. P. H. Del.

1

Introduction

THE art and science of fortification must be amongst the
earliest skills of mankind, for Man since the Fall has been
under the necessity of defending himself and his possessions
against the attacks of his neighbours. The face of this as
of any other country is marked and scarred—those who
view history as romance may prefer to say embellished—
by the fortifications of almost every race and generation
dwelling therein, not excluding our own. Seen against this
background, the castle is but one form of fortification, and
in attempting to write of its history we must begin by de-
fining it and by considering how this particular type of
fortress, the castle, which we instinctively and rightly associate with the Middle Ages, may be distinguished from
earlier and later military works.

The castle, then, was the private fortress and residence
of a lord, whether king or baron. It is this private nature
of the castle above all which principally distinguishes it
from its predecessors in the history of fortification, just as
its private and residential character serves to distinguish it
also from the purely military fortresses of more modern
times, built by governments for national defence. The
castle's predecessors in this country, the forts of the Ancient Britons, the *burhs* of the Anglo-Saxons and the Danes,
were all of them defences for a community, and Roman
fortifications, being permanent military camps and settle-
ments, have the same communal element. The essential
note is struck when a contemporary document tells us that
Ethelfleda, the daughter of King Alfred, built the *burh* of
Worcester, 'to shelter all the folk'. The Anglo-Saxon *burh*,

denoting a fortified place, is the word from which our modern *borough* derives, and in fact the *burhs* of both Saxon and Dane were fortified townships, as were also such great British fortresses as Maiden 'Castle' in Dorset and the more important Roman camps, some of which, like Lincoln, Colchester and London itself, have become in the process of time modern cities. The counterpart of these communal fortifications in the Middle Ages is the fortified or walled town of which there are many remains. But the castle, by contrast, is the private stronghold and residence of one man, his family and immediate following. The whole difference in concept and theory between communal and individual fortification is equally clear in visual fact. The Norman castle at Old Sarum is merely a citadel within the huge circumference of the far earlier encampment (1); the castle at Porchester in Hampshire comfortably occupies but one corner of the original Roman camp (2); and at Wallingford in Berkshire the site of the castle lies in one corner of the still-surviving Saxon *burh*.

The private nature of the castle is indeed the vital fact in its origin and history, wedding it firmly to the Middle Ages and that state of society which we call feudal. 'Feudal' is a vague word applied by later generations to a society which we still do not entirely understand. It is a word, moreover, which has suffered much by misuse, becoming all too often in popular history a Bad Thing, to be associated with vague ideas of the 'Dark Ages', petty tyranny and monstrous superstition; while in popular politics it has become an irritating synonym for 'reaction'. In fact, of course, feudalism was a sensible affair, developing naturally in accordance with contemporary necessity and circumstance. Its defence, if it needed one, would be simply that it worked. It is not our business here to discuss feudal society in all its aspects, and it will suffice to stress three important characteristics most relevant to our purpose. It was, in its upper levels, a military society; it was a society based upon personal lordship; and it had the political characteristic of decentralisation. The power of the state, which we are pleased to see concentrated in the central government, was diffused and distributed, to a greater or lesser extent in different realms and periods, among an hundred-and-one lords and magnates who, while owing fealty and homage, loyalty and service to their superiors on the feudal ladder, and directly or indirectly to the king, demanded and obtained in their turn the same from their own tenants and men. Feudalism has its origin on the Continent, in the Western Europe of the eighth century. With the break-up of the Carolingian Empire in the ninth century it flourished as a necessary alternative to the dwindling power of the state, and was fired in the crucible of military crisis, when Western civilisation was threatened with extinction by the inroads of the Norsemen on the one hand and the enveloping advance of the Moslem world and the incursions of the Magyars on the other. And in the growth of feudalism is found the origin of the castle—the private fortress of individual magnates and princes, providing their personal defence from the attacks of their enemies and neighbours, the symbol of their lordship and much of the substance of their power, yet providing also, in its rôle as a stronghold or a base for active operations, some measure of protection for the surrounding lands and those who dwelt within them.

While the castle was becoming a commonplace on the mainland of Western Europe by about the middle of the tenth century, and had its origin probably in the ninth, it does not appear in England until the middle of the eleventh century. England suffered no less than France from the devastating onslaughts of the Norsemen, 'who for more than two centuries filled the world with noise and fury'. But while in the Frankish kingdoms the breakdown of central governments is reflected by an edict of Charles the Bald, as early as 864, against the raising of private fortresses, in England defence against the Danes was organised on a national scale by Alfred and his successors, and the fortified centres of resistance were the *burhs*, designed like Worcester 'to shelter all the folk'. Final defeat when it came at length was also nation-wide, and the Danish Canute ruled over all England. In the absence of any serious disintegration of the state, there could be no place for the alternative organisation of petty feudal principalities and lordships which developed on the Continent, with all the attendant evils of private warfare, and the castle, the personal stronghold, remained unknown. In England the castle was introduced by the Normans, who established also in their new kingdom a highly developed form of feudal society which, controlled by the king, the lord of lords, and his powerful central government, contributed to the unification rather than the disintegration of the conquered land.

There are few chapters in European history more remarkable or more impressive than that which relates the progress and achievement of the Normans. Themselves originally numbered, as their name clearly shows, among the Norsemen whose marauding longboats were the terror of Western Europe in the ninth and tenth centuries, they had carved for themselves from the fair land of France their province of Normandy. Thus established, they adopted, adapted and improved the elements of Western civilisation which they found there, until by the time of William the Bastard, later the Conqueror and King of England, Normandy had become 'the strongest and most coherent principality in Western Europe'. From Normandy their restless energy drove them on, to conquer England, to conquer the south of Italy and establish the Norman Kingdom of Sicily, and to carry their victorious arms even beyond the limits of Europe among the leaders of the First Crusade and the founders of the Latin Kingdom of Jerusalem.

From England itself they pressed on again, northward into Scotland and westward into Wales and subsequently into Ireland. As the chronicler and poet Jordan Fantosme proudly wrote, a century after the conquest of England, 'Normans are good conquerors, there is no race like them.' For above all, this hard, ruthless, immensely efficient, proud and rather splendid race of men, excelled in the art of war, then based upon the mailed and mounted knight and upon the castle. And in this country, to which we must now confine our attention, the path of their conquest is marked by the castles which they raised.

2

Early Norman Castles

IN England the castle owes its origin to the Normans, and the history of the English castle begins to all intents and purposes with that 'memorable' date, 1066. The very few castles which are known to have existed before the Norman Conquest—Hereford, Richard's Castle and Ewyas Harold, all in Herefordshire, Clavering in Essex, and possibly Dover —were all raised in the last few years of the Old English Kingdom, in the case of Dover by Earl Harold in accordance with his oath to Duke William of Normandy, and the others by Norman adventurers already established in the land. We have seen that England in the eleventh century showed little trace of the feudal organisation of society prevalent on the Continent, and in military matters also she lagged somewhat behind contemporary developments on the other side of the Channel—the gallant and remarkable fight of Harold's army at Hastings notwithstanding. The chronicler Ordericus Vitalis, indeed, gives the lack of castles in England as one reason for the success of the Norman Conquest. Describing how King William, after his victory, traversed the country from end to end and fortified the most suitable places against the twin dangers of invasion and native risings, he adds, 'For the fortresses which the Gauls call *castella* [castles] had been very few in the English provinces: and on this account the English, although warlike and courageous, had nevertheless shown themselves too weak to withstand their enemies.'

With the coming of the Normans all this was changed. One of William's first acts on English soil, even before the decisive battle with Harold, was to build a castle at Hastings (5). Thereafter castles were raised in ever-increasing numbers throughout the length and breadth of the land as the means whereby both the king and his barons riveted their rule upon the conquered kingdom. Contemporary chronicles are full of references to the castle-building activities of the conquerors. Ordericus Vitalis, after the passage quoted above, goes on to describe how King William raised castles at Warwick, Nottingham, York, Lincoln, Cambridge and Huntingdon. The Anglo-Saxon Chronicle tells how, in February 1067, the victorious and newly crowned king crossed the Channel to visit his duchy of Normandy, leaving Bishop Odo of Bayeux and Earl William fitz Osbern behind as regents, and how they 'wrought castles widely throughout the nation, and oppressed the poor people; and ever after that it greatly grew in evil. May the end be good when God will.' The same chronicle, attempting a summary of William the Conqueror's achievements and character after his death, says simply, 'Castles he caused to be made, and poor men to be greatly oppressed.' Something of the impact of the new castles and new ways of the invader upon the old society of the Anglo-Saxons is echoed in the terse record by Domesday Book (1086) of the number of houses destroyed where castles were raised in existing towns and cities. One hundred and sixty-six houses were demolished at Lincoln to make room for the castle, and one hundred and thirteen at Norwich. Nor was it only the king and his lieutenants who caused castles to be made to defend the kingdom or the royal interests; individual barons and lords also raised their own castles, as fortresses to defend their newly acquired possessions, and as residences in which they could be safe from a potentially hostile populace. That the native chronicles should reflect hostility to the phenomenon of the English castles and associate them with oppression is scarcely surprising, for the raising of castles must often have been carried out by forced labour, while the finished results were the symbols of conquest and the strongholds of a new, alien ruling class.

In appearance the typical early Norman castle, like the earliest castles on the Continent, was far removed from the stately edifice of stone which we associate with the very word 'castle'. It employed the oldest of all methods of fortification, the earthwork, and in all save a few rare instances was devoid of any stone building, being a simple but very efficient fortress of earthwork and timber alone. While varying in detail, the vast majority of these castles conform to a basic and distinctive plan. The most prominent and most important feature was a large mound or *motte*, flattened at the top (6, 7). Where possible this mound was wholly or partially formed out of a natural hillock or outcrop of rock, but very commonly it was an entirely artificial creation, raised by what must have been a prodigious amount of spade work (5). This strongpoint was further defended by an earthen rampart or breastwork round its flat summit, and by a deep ditch round its base— the soil from the ditch being used for the raising of the mound and also for the construction of the counterscarp or earthen rampart on the outer circumference of the ditch itself. At the foot of the mound, but separated from it by its ditch, lay the *bailey*, a simple enclosure marked out and defended by its own earthen rampart and deep ditch with counterscarp. This ditch ran into the ditch of the mound so that the plan of the whole position is rather like a figure-of-eight, one segment enlarged to form the bailey.

This type of fortress is known as the *motte-and-bailey* castle from its component parts. Earthworks were its basis and most of its strength, and its simplest and most common form is that of a single mound and bailey as described above. The surviving earthworks at Berkhamsted (7), at Topcliffe (p. 25), Stafford, Tickhill and Ely are typical of the majority of castles raised immediately after the Conquest

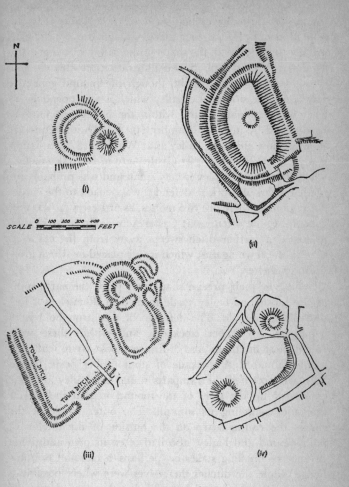

Motte-and-bailey castles: some surviving earthworks
(i) Topcliffe, Yorkshire   (ii) Bramber, Sussex
(iii) Castle Acre, Norfolk   (iv) Lewes, Sussex

and in the century which followed. The general plan of the motte-and-bailey castle was, however, capable of variation in detail. In the first place, though the mound was usually round or oval, the shape of the bailey varied greatly, as a glance at the plans and illustrations to this chapter show clearly enough. Again, though the mound generally stands on one side of the bailey which is an appendage to it, it is occasionally found within the bailey and entirely surrounded by it, as at Bramber (p. 25). Quite frequently there is more than one bailey as at Windsor (37), at Brinklow in Warwickshire, or at Castle Acre in Norfolk (p. 25), where the second bailey is very small and was probably intended as an outwork to defend the approach to the castle. Exceptionally there are two mottes, as at Lewes (p. 25) and Lincoln. Quite often, as at Castle Acre again or at Pleshey in Essex, a further ditch sweeps away from the castle to take in the town against which it was placed or which grew up in its shelter.

Whatever their precise shape and plan, the earthworks of the motte-and-bailey castle formed in themselves a formidable stronghold. The defences of this stronghold were completed by timber stockades, and within these were raised those buildings, also of timber, necessary to make the castle habitable. A stockade of stout timber posts, bound together, crowned the ramparts round the bailey and was continued up the sides of the mound to join the similar stockade encircling its summit. The outer fringe of the castle, the counterscarp on the outside of the ditches of both mound and bailey, also had often its own additional defence of bristling stakes or, perhaps, a close-set bramble hedge, while the ditches themselves were where possible—but by no means invariably—filled with water. Upon the summit of the mound and within its stockade rose usually a wooden tower, an ultimate strongpoint and vantage point of the castle by reason of its superior height, but sometimes designed also as the residence of the lord. This tower seems usually to have been raised upon posts, as is shown by recent excavations at Abinger in Surrey, and by the proud description, written in Stephen's reign (1135–54), by Laurence the Prior of Durham, of the tower upon the motte at Durham—'four posts are plain, on which it rests, one post at each strong corner'. Within the bailey were placed the other buildings necessary to the castle in its rôle as fortress, residence and, very often, the administrative centre of a district—a hall for meals, which was also the centre of social life and frequently the only accommodation for the lord's retainers and garrison, a chapel, stables, storehouses and barns, and perhaps a kitchen in those establishments where cooking was not done out of doors. Entrance to the castle was gained by a wooden bridge, probably some form of drawbridge, over the ditch of the bailey, and by a gateway in the stockade, made as strong as possible and often further defended by wooden towers. Communication between the mound, surrounded by its own ditch, and the bailey, was provided generally by a sloping bridge carried on piles, which again at some point could be raised or blocked in case of attack.

The dominant feature of these fortresses was the motte or mound, designed as the strongest point, a separate citadel within the castle, capable of separate and independent defence. We shall see later that repeatedly in siege-warfare, if the attackers succeeded in taking the bailey, the defenders withdrew to the mound and continued their resistance there, and we may notice also here that, since the mound stood to one side of the bailey, the garrison in such circumstances had in the last resort some chance of escaping to the open country at their back. The mound also, by virtue both of its military strength and lofty eminence, might bear the residence of the lord of the castle. It is perhaps possible that occasionally the earliest castles consisted of a motte alone without any adjacent bailey, and certain that very few were raised without any motte. The only early castles which could dispense with this invaluable citadel were either those rare examples, like the Peak in Derbyshire or Bamburgh, built upon a site which was itself wholly elevated and almost impregnable, or those equally rare, like Colchester and the Tower of London (27), which had almost from the beginning a great stone keep. In the latter case, as we shall see in the next chapter, the tower keeps merely reproduced and augmented all the advantages of the motte as a self-sufficient strongpoint designed for ultimate defence. In height the motte is generally from twenty to thirty feet, though occasionally it rises much higher like the great hundred-foot Castle Hill at Thetford in Norfolk (6). In area the motte is much smaller than the bailey, and the whole area of the castle, it must be emphasised again, is comparatively small—usually not above three acres and often not more than one and a half—in sharp distinction to earlier pre-Norman fortifications and as befits the private fortress and residence of an individual lord and his immediate following.

We must not be misled by the simplicity of the early castle, as compared with the elaborate stone castle of a later age, into doubting its efficiency. Professor Hamilton Thompson pointed out long ago that if, as has been the case in colonial warfare, a stockaded enclosure can be an effective barrier to modern troops equipped with firearms, the barrier which the motte-and-bailey castle presented to the early medieval warrior may easily be imagined. Such castles in fact were formidable strongholds. They were a sufficient answer to the cavalry of mailed knights which then dominated open warfare, and their deep ditches, steep banks and stout palisades made an attack on foot a difficult and hazardous operation. Their mounds especially were extremely difficult to assault—as anyone who even now climbs one may prove for himself. In addition, they were quick and easy to construct, and this above all made them especially suited to the needs of the Norman conquerors of England.

Of these early Norman castles of earth and timber we have not only contemporary written descriptions but even contemporary pictures. The unique and invaluable pictorial record of the Norman Conquest preserved in the Bayeux Tapestry shows clearly, though with some artistic license and a charming lack of perspective and proportion, the towered and palisaded mounds of the castles at Dol, Rennes, Dinan and Bayeux in Normandy, and shows also the raising of Hastings Castle on Duke William's order in a way that leaves no doubt that there the mound was an artificial structure (3, 5). The fact that we possess a contemporary illustration of the building of one of the earliest English castles and the first of the many to be raised by the Conqueror in England is indeed remarkable. Among the many references of varying detail to the motte-and-bailey castle in the chronicles of the time, the two best and fullest descriptions occur in Continental works and refer to Continental castles. The first passage occurs in a twelfth-century biography of Bishop John of Terouenne by John de Colmieu, written about 1130. 'Bishop John', we are informed, 'used to stay frequently at Merchem when he was going round his diocese. Near the churchyard was an exceedingly high fortification, which might be called a castle or *municipium*, built according to the fashion of the country by the lord of the manor many years before. For it is the custom of the nobles of that region, who spend their time for the most part in private war, in order to defend themselves from their enemies, to make a hill of earth as high as they can, and encircle it with a ditch as broad and deep as possible. They surround the upper edge of this hill with a very strong wall of hewn logs, placing [small] towers on the circuit, according to their means. Inside this wall they plant their house or keep, which overlooks the whole thing. The entrance to this fortress is only by a bridge, which rises from the counterscarp of the ditch, supported on double or even triple columns, till it reaches the upper edge of the motte.' The chronicler goes on to relate the grievous tale of how one day this wooden bridge collapsed under the weight of the bishop and the press of people who followed him, and all fell some thirty-five feet into the waters of the ditch below.

That the timber tower upon the motte was not necessarily a rude and simple affair is shown by the second passage, a detailed description by Lambert of Ardres of the exceptionally elaborate structure at the castle of Ardres built about 1117. 'Arnold, lord of Ardres, built on the motte of Ardres a wooden house, excelling all the houses of Flanders of that period both in material and in carpenter's work. The first storey was on the surface of the ground, where were cellars and granaries, and great boxes, tuns, casks, and other domestic utensils. In the storey above were the dwelling and common living-rooms of the residents, in which were the larders, the rooms of the bakers and butlers, and the great chamber in which the lord and his wife slept. Adjoining this was a private room, the dormitory of the waiting maids and children. In the inner part of the great chamber was a certain private room, where at early dawn or in the evening or during sickness or at time of blood-letting, or for warming the maids and weaned children, they used to have a fire. ... In the upper storey of the house were garret rooms, in which on the one side the sons (when they wished it), on the other side the daughters (because they were obliged), of the lord of the house used to sleep. In this storey also the watchmen and the servants appointed to keep the house took their sleep at some time or other. High up on the east side of the house, in a convenient place, was the chapel, which was made like unto the tabernacle of Solomon in its ceiling and painting. There were stairs and passages from storey to storey, from the house into the kitchen, from room to room, and again from the house into the loggia, where they used to sit in conversation for recreation, and again from the loggia into the oratory.'

It may be noticed that in neither of the contemporary descriptions quoted, nor in the Bayeux Tapestry, is there any mention or sign of the bailey, but this should be taken as an implication of the immense importance, both militarily and socially, of the motte in the whole design of the castle, rather than as an indication that the bailey was commonly dispensed with. However large the mound, the space upon its summit was confined, and was further limited by the timber tower or other dwelling upon it. The bailey must in almost every case have been essential for all the necessary appendages of a feudal household—barns, stables, smithies and, no doubt, a hall for its common life —while in war it was no less important as an outwork to the mound, providing space and accommodation for the garrison, their horses and some at least of their supplies, and affording shelter too, perhaps, for livestock brought in from the surrounding lands.

Taken in all, even the rich evidence of contemporary written descriptions and illustrations of these early castles is little compared with the wealth of archaeological evidence that surrounds us on every side. We have seen that in the Conqueror's reign castles were raised in large numbers by both the king and his magnates. The process was continued under his immediate successors, and was accelerated in the troubled reign of Stephen (1135–54) when, in the words of the Anglo-Saxon Chronicle, 'They filled the land full of castles.' The planting of castles was not confined merely to cities which had to be overawed, to the frontier areas of the south-east coast and the northern and western marches, nor to the lines which mark the Norman incursions into Scotland and into Wales. They were raised also in every part of the country and in every shire, for where a great man had lands which he wished to visit, there as like as not he built a castle as his fortified residence. There were more castles in England in the first century after the Conquest than at any later time, and the great majority of our castles have their origins in this period. What is more, most of this extensive Norman fortification still remains for those who care to see. Many of these early strongholds were later converted into stone fortresses, and in consequence at many of our finest surviving castles, at Windsor (37) for example, or at Warwick, Arundel or Durham, the original motte-and-bailey form and foundation may clearly be seen beneath the accumulated stonework of after years. At other sites, like Berkhamsted in Hertfordshire (7), the later stonework has now almost gone, leaving the original earthworks exposed much as they were first dug and scarped. At many others yet again, early abandoned and perhaps therefore never fortified in stone, the unmistakable mounds at least, and often the lines of ditches and ramparts, still triumphantly survive. There is scarcely any district which cannot show the remains of its early castles, and their uncounted numbers are by far the most numerous memorials of the Anglo-Norman kingdom, as they are also the most dramatic evidence for the coming of the Normans into England and the type of society which they there established.

That it was introduced into this country by the Normans and that in its earliest form it was almost invariably a stronghold of earthwork and timber—these are the first basic facts in the history of the English castle. Yet neither was generally realised by historians and archaeologists until

1   Old Sarum, Wiltshire: the Norman castle within the ancient British earthwork. (The foundations of the Norman cathedral, subsequently removed to the new Salisbury, can also be seen)

2   Porchester, Hampshire: the medieval castle occupies but one corner of the Roman camp

PVG[NA]NT : CONTRA DINANTES

3 (above) The castle
    at Dinan

HIC HAR

4 (left) Harold and
  his friends in the
  hall at Bosham

5 (below) The rais-
  ing of the motte
  at Hastings, 1066

[V]TL[O]DERETVR : CASTELLVM : A[T] HESTENG[A] CEASTRA

6 Thetford, Norfolk: the great motte of the castle

7 Berkhamsted, Hertfordshire: the later stonework has almost vanished to reveal the eleventh-century earthworks of the motte-and-bailey castle

8 Castle Rising, Norfolk: the mid-twelfth-century keep of the Albini earls of Sussex standing within the vast Norman earthworks

9 Rochester, Kent (c. 1130), showing the thirteenth-century angle tower in the centre and the forebuilding on the right

10 Castle Hedingham, Essex (c. 1140). Note the ruins of the forebuilding in the left foreground (cf. pages 46-7)

12 (above) Conisborough, Yorkshire: the keep (c. 1190) of the Warenne earls of Surrey (cf. p. 53)

11 (left) Orford, Suffolk: the keep (1165-73)

13 Pembroke: the splendid cylindrical keep (*c.* 1200) of William Marshal, earl of Pembroke, dominates the castle

14 Restormel, Cornwall: a large shell keep upon a mound

15 Clifford's Tower, York: the thirteenth-century quatrefoil tower keep upon the eleventh-century castle mound

the present century. Learned ignorance and popular fancy combined to produce that unhappy state of affairs in which 'one earthwork was as good as another'. So great was the confusion that a vast British earthwork in Dorset has become for all time Maiden *Castle,* while innumerable small mounds and enclosures, the authentic survivals of early castles, were not recognised as castles at all. Now, thanks to the tireless efforts of Mrs. Ella Armitage, the inspired pugnacity of John Horace Round, and the judicious exposition of Alexander Hamilton Thompson, these things are better understood. Yet even now the fact that a castle need not be, and for some hundred years in this country alone was often not, a fortress of stone, is anything but common knowledge. So numerous are the remains of early castles that few need travel far to find one. But when the locality is reached little help can be expected from the inhabitants of the town or village. To the question 'Where is the castle?' comes the answer pat, 'There is no castle here', so deep-rooted and widespread is the conviction that a castle can only be a building or ruin of stone. Many are the stories, sad but instructive, that could be told along these lines, but the best which comes to mind concerns a certain pleasant town in Shropshire. There, soon after the Norman Conquest, close on nine hundred years ago, a castle was founded which long survived and played a not unimportant part in the warfare of the Welsh Marches, the unruly borderlands between England and Wales. As is so often the case, the motte forms its principal remains today, a large and lofty mound which still dominates the town. Having toiled to the top of this with a mildly protesting uncle, I found its flat summit laid out as a bowling-green. Since the green was private I thought it best to atone for my trespass by polite conversation with an adjacent member. I commented on the fineness of the weather, praised the fineness of the turf, and remarked how odd it was to think that this was once a castle. He looked put out, and replied with authority that there had never been a castle here, for it had been a bowling-green as long as ever he could remember. This was subsequently confirmed by the oldest inhabitant.

3

Early Stone Castles

THE architectural history of the English castle is usually one of continuous development from an early origin—followed, of course, all too often, by continous or rapid decline. Although in all later periods of the Middle Ages some entirely new fortresses were raised, incorporating at the outset the most recent advances in military architecture, such instances are comparatively few, and the majority of English castles were founded in the first century after the Norman Conquest. Thereafter their development was continuous and slow, so that the typical castle which we see, whether ruined or complete, is the combined result of the changing needs and skills of many generations.

Perhaps the most striking development in the evolution of the English castle was the change from the stronghold of earthwork and timber to the fortress of stone. The type of early castle which we examined in the last chapter was by no means confined to this country. Similar needs, similar patterns of society and similar resources produced the same results elsewhere, and fortification in earthwork and timber was common to all feudal Europe in the eleventh century. At the same time it may readily be seen that the motte-and-bailey castle, by virtue of the speed and ease with which it could be constructed, was exactly suited to the Norman conquerors of England, whose needs were to consolidate the victory of Hastings without delay, to hold what they had won, and to impose their rule upon a potentially hostile populace. It is significant that when, a century later, the Anglo-Normans under Henry II pushed on to the conquest of Ireland, they raised there the same familiar type

of motte-and-bailey fortress which was then already obso-
lescent in England. However, we know the Normans to
have been energetic builders in stone from their churches,
and if the mighty pile of Durham Cathedral above the
Wear were the sole monument remaining to them we
should know them to have been highly skilled in the mason's art. It was inevitable that as the first urgency of the
Conquest declined, and the resources of both king and
baronage increased, they should have sought for their castles
the greater strength, permanence and comfort which stone
could provide. Further, the transition from the castle of
earthwork and timber to the castle of stone, in England
as on the Continent, was the effect as well as the cause of
the adoption during the twelfth century of improved methods of siege-craft and more powerful siege-engines.

The transition was, however, both slow and piecemeal.
Both record and archaeological evidence leave no doubt
that it was most concentrated in the second half of the
twelfth century. Then, for example, the surviving series of
the Pipe Rolls, the annual rolls of the Exchequer which
record the greater part of royal expenditure, show the king
each year disbursing large sums upon castle-building. We
know, chiefly from archaeological evidence, both that this
building was in stone, and that the barons no less than the
king were fortifying their castles after the same fashion.
Yet the transition extends also on both sides of that period.
Fortification of the older and simpler kind survived throughout it and well into the thirteenth century. Thus the mound
at York continued to be crowned with a timber tower until
the present remarkable stone keep (15) was built by Henry
III between 1245 and 1272. Until at least the early years
of the thirteenth century strongholds of earth and timber
continued even to be newly raised in times of emergency
and civil war. On the other hand, examples of the stone
fortification which only became general in the second half

of the twelfth century can be found long before. The stone keeps of Canterbury, Carlisle, Corfe, Norwich, Rochester (9) and Castle Hedingham (10) all belong to the first half of that century, and, most remarkable of all, the great keeps of Colchester and the Tower of London (27) were raised by order of the Conqueror himself. Stone fortification in eleventh-century England is altogether exceptional, but to the examples of the Conqueror's massive keeps at Colchester and the Tower we may probably add the keeps at Bramber and at Pevensey, and certainly the early Norman stonework still to be seen in the walls and other buildings of Ludlow, Rochester, Richmond and the Peak. Such exceptional cases presuppose exceptional causes. The two castles last named both stood upon rocky sites which made the normal ditch, bank and mound impossible to dig, and thus made necessary at least a stone wall as a perimeter defence. Bramber, Pevensey and Colchester probably owe the early strength of their stone keeps to their particular rôle as defences against invasion, and the great Tower of London scarcely needs any other cause than the importance of that city.

The most usual type of early stone castle, which we may roughly assign to the second half of the twelfth and first half of the thirteenth centuries when it was most common, is best described as the *keep-and-bailey* castle. Generally it was not only the immediate successor of the motte-and-bailey, but literally grew out of it, for the great majority of stone castles were raised upon the sites of existing strongholds, stone walls and buildings gradually replacing the timber stockades and buildings of the original. It was, therefore, the medium rather than the underlying theory of fortification which was changed. The keep-and-bailey castle, like the motte-and-bailey, consisted of the same two component parts in the same relation to each other—the bailey, now a walled enclosure, and a citadel, now the stone keep, which either incorporated or replaced the existing mound.

The bailey itself in the new stone castles need not detain us long. Some of the earliest stone fortification, we have seen, is found in the bailey walls of certain castles sited upon rocky and elevated sites, like Richmond or the Peak, where the building of a wall as the only possible form of perimeter defence was demanded from the outset. Much more frequently, however, the bailey wall was added later to an existing motte-and-bailey fortress. It was raised along the crest of the original ramparts round the bailey, and simply replaced the timber stockade which had previously stood there. As before, the defences of the bailey were completed by the surrounding ditch, wet or dry, with its counterscarp. From a very early date the top of the wall was broken up by *crenellation* or battlements, with a corresponding platform (*alatorium* in Latin from which is derived the technical word *allure* for a rampart walk) on the inside to enable the garrison actively to defend the castle (p. 71).

Particular attention was paid to the fortification of the gateway, which as the principal or only entrance to the castle was always a possible weak point, and one which generally received the first and most concentrated attentions of the besiegers. The obvious necessity of strongly fortifying the entrance led to the building, sometimes at a very early date, of stone gatehouses. The earliest examples, found at those castles provided from the first with bailey walls, are usually in form a broad square tower containing the gate. One of the earliest known survivals of this type is the fine gatehouse at Exeter dating from the eleventh century, while at both Richmond and Ludlow similar early gatehouses were converted during the twelfth century into tower keeps by blocking the entrance passage and adding additional storeys. In the twelfth century we find an alternative method of fortifying the castle gate by building stone towers against the bailey wall on either side of it. This was the method adopted by Henry II at Dover (36), where the twin towers, placed one on either side of each of the two entrances to the inner bailey, are not the least remarkable features of that remarkable work. The particular attention paid to the defence of the gate in this as in all periods of the Middle Ages provides us with one small but precise example of the general transition from timber to stone fortification. A letter of King John to the sheriff of Worcester, dated 1204, orders the rebuilding at Worcester Castle of the gateway 'which is now of wood, with good and fine stone'.

Within the bailey, as before, but now of stone, stood the 'houses in the castle', as contemporary records call them, that is to say those miscellaneous buildings necessary to the castle in its rôle both as residence and fortress. Most often they comprised at least a chapel, a hall, storehouses and stables, and were commonly ranged against the bailey wall, thus being sheltered while leaving the centre of the enclosure free. Amongst them the hall and the chapel were the most important, though as a result of their very importance, together with the continual development and improvement of most castles during the Middle Ages, fewer early examples have survived than could be wished. Our medieval ancestors, it may be noted, were severely practical and had little feeling about the preservation of ancient monuments. The chapel appears often to have been the first building in the castle to have achieved the dignity of stone. One of the earliest surviving examples is the breath-taking little early Norman chapel at Durham (44), recently and excellently restored by the University and a fitting gem for one of our finest surviving episcopal castles. Its date must be placed in the 1070s, and the grotesque carving of its capitals seems to suggest a native craftsmanship reaching back yet earlier to the days before the coming of the Normans.

39

Another early chapel, probably of the eleventh century, survives at Richmond, and Ludlow contains the fine and substantial remains of a twelfth-century chapel, particularly interesting in its circular plan, standing within the bailey of the castle (45).

The hall was the most important secular building within the bailey and the centre of normal domestic life at least for the garrison. In plan the great hall changed very little throughout the Middle Ages, whether it stood within the

Boothby Pagnell, Lincolnshire: the twelfth-century hall

fortifications of a castle, or elsewhere as the centre and nucleus of an unfortified manor-house (above). The stone halls of the twelfth and thirteenth centuries differ in no important respects save building materials from the timber halls of the eleventh century, such as that in which Harold and his friends are shown feasting in the Bayeux Tapestry (4); the early stone halls of the twelfth and thirteenth centuries, in turn, differ little from the more spacious halls of the later Middle Ages—at Caerphilly, Warwick or Kenilworth—or indeed from the halls of Oxford and Cambridge colleges. In the castle the great hall was the place for food and drink and feasting, and for all forms of social or administrative activity. Moreover, in the sparse domestic arrangements of early castles it must have afforded almost the only shelter for the garrison and serving men, who slept in it and probably used it as a general barrack-room as well. Its basic plan was simple. The main apartment, or hall proper, which occupied almost the entire length, often stood over a basement or undercroft, used for storage. At one end was the entrance which also led to the kitchens if any, though in the early castles cooking seems generally to have been done out of doors. At the opposite end was a dais upon which the table of the lord was set at right angles to the body of the hall. Beyond the dais and set apart by a partition wall there was usually the great chamber, where the lord and his lady might withdraw to rest and sleep in the rare luxury of privacy. Amongst the few early survivals pride of place must go to the almost perfect eleventh-century stone hall, again at Richmond in Yorkshire. The remains of a late twelfth-century hall (in form one large apartment with no great chamber) still stand at Christchurch in Hampshire, while the very fine hall at Oakham in Rutlandshire (48) is an almost pefect specimen of the same date. Perhaps the finest of all early medieval halls, however, is that at Winchester, now all that remains of a castle once the favoured residence of our kings. Though a twelfth-century foundation, this hall owes its present appearance to the lavish care bestowed upon it by Henry III (49).

So much, then, for the bailey, which is now defended by a stone wall and gateway as well as by its ditch and earthen ramparts, and contains the hall, chapel and other stone buildings, 'the houses in the castle', ranged along one or more of its sides. But the most important part of the early stone castle from the military, and usually from the residential, point of view was the keep. The keep was designed as the strongest point of the castle, and, more than this, as a separate and self-sufficient unit within it, capable of separate and successful defence should the rest of the castle be taken. It was also, in the great majority of cases, the residence of the lord of the castle. The keep of the keep-and-bailey castle, therefore, had exactly the same rôle as the motte of the motte-and-bailey, and indeed it was upon the motte that the simplest form of keep was invariably placed, its stonework replacing the earlier timber fortification. The stockade formerly planted upon the earthen rampart which surrounded the flat summit of the mound was simply replaced by a stone wall. This type of ring wall crowning a mound is known as a shell keep. It was linked to the defences of the bailey, for the bailey wall was continued up the two sides of the motte, just as the older stockades had been, to join the shell wall at two points. Within the strong enclosure of the new and embattled wall, and upon the summit of the motte, the old timber tower-house was in due course replaced by such stone buildings as were necessary either to the residence of the lord or to the defence of the keep. They, like the houses in the bailey, were ranged against the inside of the wall so that the centre of the small elevated enclosure was left free. At Southampton in 1187 the Pipe Roll refers to the building of the king's chambers upon the castle mound. We know from later records that the shell keep which Henry II probably raised upon the mound at Windsor contained hall, chambers and probably a chapel. As late as the reign of Edward III (1327 –77) these buildings were replaced by a new range, which still survives, built of timber all round the inside of the shell wall, leaving an open courtyard in the centre. Windsor, indeed, though the encircling wall has been much restored, heightened and provided with uncompromisingly nineteenth-century windows, still affords one of the finest surviving examples of the shell keep, clearly in its dominating position upon the mound the strongpoint of the castle, and capable of a not uncomfortable defence (37). A good visual impression of this type of keep can also be obtained from an aerial photograph of Restormel in Cornwall, whose present remains are of a large shell upon a mound, its crenellated wall still near perfect and still containing the substantial remains of the stone buildings round its inner face (14). Other excellent examples are found at Arundel, Tamworth, Trematon, Cardiff and Carisbrooke, while elsewhere the summit of many an abandoned mound is still marked by the ruins or foundations of former shells. The splendid keep at Berkeley and the ruined keep at Farnham are rare examples of an uncommon alternative arrangement, whereby the shell wall, instead of being built round the summit of the motte, is built round its base, and is then carried up as a revetment to the whole mound.

The shell keep is a common feature of the English castle both because it could most easily be added to an existing motte-and-bailey stronghold and because it was also reasonably cheap to construct. Nevertheless another type of keep, the tower keep, stands as the classic feature of the early stone castle and remains perhaps the most striking legacy of English medieval military architecture. In its best-known and most usual rectangular form, the tower keep is associated especially with the later twelfth century. King Henry II himself was an energetic builder of them, and built the keeps of Scarborough and the Peak, Bridgenorth, Newcastle-on-Tyne and Dover (p. 49; 36), as well as completing those of Bamburgh, Bowes and Richmond. But though the tower keep is particularly and rightly associated with this period, and was then added to so many castles up and down the land or raised as the principal strength and centre of those then newly built, as a form af military architecture it spans much of the entire Middle Ages. Such

43

keeps as those at Canterbury, Carlisle, Corfe, Norwich, Rochester (9) and Castle Hedingham (10) we have already seen to belong to the earlier twelfth century, and Colchester and the Tower of London (27) to the earliest years of the Norman Conquest. On the other hand the keeps of Pembroke (13), Caldicott or Launceston, in their improved cylindrical shape, belong to the thirteenth century, while to the very end of the castle's active history rectangular tower keeps, or something very like them, continued to be built. Nor upon reflection is this longevity surprising, for basically the strong tower was, after all, the simple and logical answer to the problem of providing, in one compact building, a residence which should also be capable of sustained defence and be as near impregnable as military science could make it.

In form a massive rectangular tower, the outward appearance of the typical rectangular tower keep of the twelfth century is sufficiently shown by photographs of Dover (36), Castle Hedingham (10), Rochester (9) and Castle Rising (8). It is clear at a glance that defence, and chiefly passive defence, was the overwhelming consideration in design and construction. The stout walls are generally, save in the earliest keeps, splayed out to form a plinth at the base, where they were exposed to the picks, bores, battering rams and other machinations of the attackers. Thereafter the tower rises sheer to the summit, and the kind of external ornament which is found at Norwich and Castle Rising is quite exceptional. Pilaster buttresses strengthen it at the corners, and these are continued above the line of the roof to form four angle turrets. One or more shallow pilaster buttresses also generally run up the faces of the tower between the angles, as may be seen, for example, at Rochester. The window openings, where the original arrangements have not suffered later alterations, are for obvious reasons both few and small, especially at the lower levels.

The entrance to the keep, also for obvious reasons, is very seldom on the ground level, and most usually leads into the first storey, though occasionally into the second. It is approached by an external staircase at right angles to it, built up the face of the wall, and the whole is covered by a fore-building, clearly visible in our illustrations of Rochester (9) and Castle Rising (8).

The strength of such keeps lay principally in their solidity. Their walls of solid masonry, constructed of rag stone or rubble encased, save in a few early instances, with outer faces of ashlar or dressed stone, were enormously thick. At Dover (p. 49) the walls of Henry II's great keep are from twenty-one to twenty-four feet wide; at Newcastle they measure fourteen feet at first-floor level; at Rochester they are twelve feet at the base and ten at the top. A slight reduction of their thickness at the upper and safer levels was usually effected by rebatement on the inside, so that both some economy of stone and some gain of internal space were achieved at one and the same time. The overall dimensions of the square tower keeps, of course, vary from place to place. At Colchester, the largest of them all, the area covered measures one hundred and fifty-two feet by one hundred and eleven; the height may no longer be determined since the upper storeys have now disappeared. The White Tower at London (27) rivals Colchester, measuring one hundred and eighteen feet by one hundred and seven in length and breadth, while its height is some ninety feet. Both these keeps are exceptionally early and nothing quite on their scale was later attempted—possibly because, whereas most twelfth-century keeps were added to existing fortified sites, these two eleventh-century examples were raised immediately after the Conquest and must originally have formed almost the entire strength of their respective cestles. The keep at Dover, the finest of all the twelfth-century keeps and also, so far as we know, the most

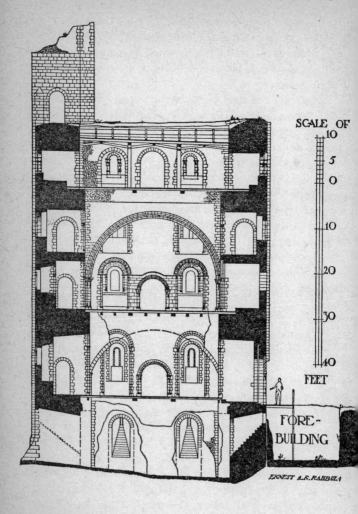

SCALE OF

10

5

0

10

20

30

40

FEET

FORE-
BUILDING

ERNEST A.R.RAHBULA

Castle Hedingham, Essex: section through keep (cf. Figure 10)

46

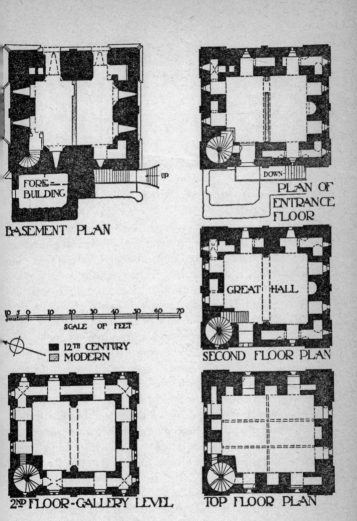

BASEMENT PLAN

FORE-BUILDING

UP

PLAN OF ENTRANCE FLOOR

DOWN

GREAT HALL

SECOND FLOOR PLAN

10 5 0   10   20   30   40   50   60   70
SCALE OF FEET

■ 12TH CENTURY
▨ MODERN

2ND FLOOR-GALLERY LEVEL

TOP FLOOR PLAN

Castle Hedingham, Essex: the keep, c. 1140 (cf. Figure 10)

47

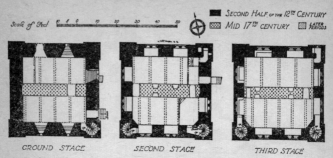

SECOND HALF OF THE 12TH CENTURY
MID 17TH CENTURY   LATER PERIODS

GROUND STAGE   SECOND STAGE   THIRD STAGE

Appleby, Westmorland: the late twelfth-century keep

expensive, measuring ninety-eight feet by ninety-six feet at
the base, and is some eighty feet high. The more modest
but very fine keep at Bamburgh, roughly contemporary in
date, measures sixty-nine feet by sixty-one in area but is
only fifty-five feet high. It will be noticed that both at
Bamburgh and Dover the height is less than either the
length or breadth, and we can in fact broadly distinguish
between keeps of this type, which are aften markedly oblong in shape, like Castle Rising (8), Kenilworth and
Middleham, and the towers proper whose height is the
greatest dimension, like Richmond, Rochester (9), Castle
Hedingham (p. 46; 10) or Porchester (2).

The internal arrangements of the tower keeps are also
variable and are largely determined by their respective sizes
and proportions. The larger keeps are divided laterally by
a cross-wall, which is not always placed centrally. From the
constructional point of view the cross-wall gave further
strength to the whole building and facilitated both the flooring of the various storeys and the final roofing where the
span would otherwise be too great. The additional structural strength provided by the cross-wall might also be of

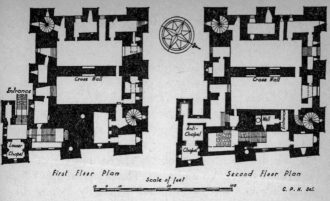

First Floor Plan   Scale of feet   Second Floor Plan

C. P. N. Del.

Dover, Kent: the keep, *c.* 1179–91 (cf. Figure 36)

direct military advantage, as is dramatically shown by one incident in the history of Rochester. King John, besieging the castle in 1215, succeeded after much labour in bringing down one corner of the keep by mining, and thus forced an entry. The defenders, however, withdrew behind the cross-wall and continued for a space their stubborn resistance in the other half of the tower. The vertical division of the loftier tower keeps was commonly into a basement and three upper floors, as at Hedingham (p. 46), Rochester or Porchester. Both Guilford and Corfe, however, have only two upper floors, while at Norham there are four. At Castle Rising, Kenilworth and Middleham, all examples of the squatter, oblong type of keep, there is only a basement and one main upper floor.

After this great gap of time we cannot be too precise about the actual domestic arrangements within the keep, though some sort of picture may be pieced together by surviving architectural remains, scraps of written evidence, and surmise. An impression of the physical internal arrangement of three typical square tower keeps is provided by our plans of Dover and Appleby and from a cross-section and plans of the rather earlier tower at Hedingham (pp. 46–9). It may be worth mentioning that though the keep at Dover was built by Henry II, while Castle Hedingham was the stronghold of the de Vere earls of Oxford, there is no architectural sign of any differing social status. The king was the greatest of his magnates and his magnates lived like kings. To revert, each floor in the tower keep was basically designed as one large apartment, though it might be divided wholly or partly into two by the cross-wall. The basement was probably always used for the storage both of provisions and arms. The principal upper floor formed the hall for the lord and his family. Where there was more than one upper floor, the first was probably given over to the garrison, or to administrative business in peace, while the second was the hall. Where there was a floor above the hall it may have been divided by partitions into private chambers, as seems to have been the case at Hedingham. Sometimes, as at Hedingham and Dover, the second and third floors are combined to produce a very lofty hall, with a mural gallery surrounding its upper levels. The inconvenience of having the hall or principal rooms divided into two by the cross-wall is overcome by piercing it with arcades at Rochester and by replacing it with great transverse arches at Hedingham. The most important upper storeys of most tower keeps have fireplaces, and many keeps provide very excellent early medieval specimens. We may notice that the provision or non-provision of fireplaces is no indication of date, for eleventh-century Colchester has them while Henry II's keep at the Peak, built almost a century later, has none. Where there are no fireplaces we may probably assume the main apartments to have been warmed by a brazier standing on the floor.

Communication between the various floors was provided by one or more spiral staircases in one or more of the angles of the keep, and such staircases were continued up into the angle turrets to give access to the roof. Within the great thickness of the walls, in the upper levels of the keep, small private chambers were frequently constructed, in which the head of the household and its more favoured members might sleep. Dover in particular was well supplied with such chambers, as our plans clearly show. The walls also generally accommodated in their ample width the latrines, which were usually designed with sufficient care, skill and workmanship to give the lie to those would-be realists who imagine sanitation to be the invention of Disraeli in the nineteenth century. Lastly, the tower keeps contained a chapel and a well. The latter was vital to a building which might be closely invested for long periods, and we may assume it to have been an essential feature of every keep whether it now survives or not. Where it has survived, the precision and sheer, smooth rotundity of its deep shaft are often a striking tribute to medieval engineering skill. In some cases the only access to it was in the basement; in others, far more conveniently, the shaft was continued up into the residential floors. The chapel was also essential to a garrison cut off in war, and in peace was a convenient place of private worship for the lord and his family residing in the keep. At the Tower of London (27) and at Colchester spacious chapels were worked into the main body of the tower itself to form one more exceptional feature of these exceptional keeps. The most common arrangement in the later keeps of the twelfth century is to place a smaller chapel in the upper storey of the forebuilding over the entrance staircase. But wherever it is placed, the chapel frequently shows a degree of simple but finely worked ornamentation in contrast to the somewhat spartan lack of decoration in the rest of the tower keep.

Before leaving the tower keeps we must notice an important change which begins to appear in their design in the later twelfth century—though the importance of the

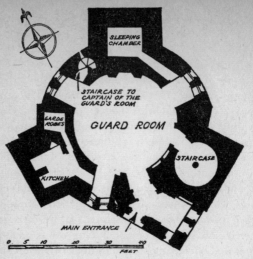

Orford, Suffolk: first storey of the keep,
c. 1165–73 (cf. Figure 11)

change lies more in the principle of military architecture
involved than in the actual number of keeps built in accordance with the new principle. From a military point of
view, the one inherent weakness in the enormous strength
of the square tower keep lay in its very shape. The stones of
its sharp angles could be worked away by attackers wielding pick and bore, while the same dangerous corners were
blind spots more or less incapable of being covered, save
from directly above, by the defenders inside the square and
sheer tower. The answer to the problem was to be the cylindrical tower keep. But as precursors of the round tower
itself, we have several instances of keeps which are transitional—polygonal keeps of many sides and therefore no
sharp angles to invite attack. The most interesting of these
is at Orford (11) on the Suffolk coast, where there still
stands in near perfect condition one of the most remark-

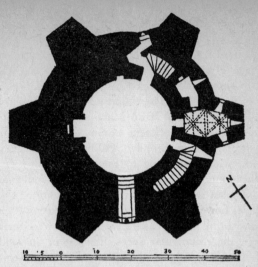

Conisborough, Yorkshire: third storey of the keep,
c. 1190 (cf. Figure 12)

able keeps in England. Orford keep, raised by Henry II
between 1165 and 1173, is cylindrical inside but polygonal
outside, the whole being strengthened and supported by
three great buttress towers built against every fifth outer
face. The keep at Chilham, built in the 1170s, again by
Henry II, is a more or less straightforward octagon in plan,
and some thirty years later King John also built an octa-
gonal keep, now much ruined, in his new castle at Odiham
in Hampshire. One of the most striking of these transitional
keeps is that at Conisborough (12) in Yorkshire, built by
a great subject of the Crown, earl Hamelin de Warenne,
halfbrother to King Henry II, in the last few years of the
twelfth century. Here the perfect cylindrical plan is almost
attained, but is marred at the last moment by the six great
buttresses which support the massive fabric of the keep.

Cylindrical tower keeps proper are principally confined

to the earlier thirteenth century, and also—though Launceston in Cornwall, New Buckenham in Norfolk, and Barnard Castle, county Durham, are splendid exceptions—to Wales, where perhaps the chronic warfare of the Marches helped to ensure the adoption of the most advanced techniques of fortification. The round keep at Pembroke (13), built about 1200 by William Marshal, earl of Pembroke, is among the finest specimens extant. Others still stand in whole or in part at Bronllys, Caldicott, Dolbadarn and Skenfrith, while, returning to England, we must bracket with the round tower its striking elaboration into the quatrefoil plan which is best illustrated at York (15). On the whole, however, the cylindrical tower keeps are not a common feature of our castles, for not only were their predecessors, the rectangular keeps, the first in the field and strong enough to remain there, but also at the very time when the advantages of the cylindrical plan were beginning to be applied to it, the keep as an ultimate strongpoint was becoming unnecessary in the greater castles by reason of other and more sweeping developments in the art and science of military architecture.

After this discussion of its several features, it now only remains to say a little of the early stone castle as a whole. We have already stressed that in the great majority of cases it grew out of the motte-and-bailey castle, stonework simply replacing the former stockades and timber buildings upon the original site. Windsor (37), for example, was thus 'converted' in the reign of Henry II, whose work there included the enclosure by stone walls of the upper bailey and part of the lower bailey, a new royal lodging built in stone within the former, and, probably, the building of the shell keep upon the mound. The early stone castle often retains, therefore, even the lay-out and the plan of its predecessor. Especially is this true of those castles with shell keeps, for the shell was invariably placed upon the existing mound, which formed indeed an essential part of it. The tower keep also, when added to an existing castle, was not infrequently placed upon the mound, especially if the mound was large, or wholly or partly natural, as at Norwich, Castle Hedingham or Clitheroe. The later cylindrical keeps, too, perhaps aided by their shape, are quite commonly placed upon a mound, as at Launceston, Longtown or Skenfrith. Often, however, the great weight of the tower keep, together with the shape of the common rectangular type, made it quite unsuitable for such a position. Sometimes the problem was solved by forceful adaptation. At Guildford and Clun the keeps are built on one side of the mound; at Kenilworth the great tower keep of the Clintons appears to have been built over and engulfed the mound; in all three cases the object was, of course, to set the foundations upon firm ground. At Rochester and Newcastle upon Tyne, on the other hand, when the tower keep was built the old mound was abandoned, and the same practice must often have been followed elsewhere. Where the tower keep does not stand upon a mound it commonly stands within the enclosure of the bailey, as at Rochester, or upon the cross-wall dividing two baileys as was originally the case at Bamburgh and Scarborough. New castles raised in the late twelfth and early thirteenth centuries with tower keeps follow the same arrangement, for certainly the massive weight of the keep could never be placed upon the insecure foundation of a newly dug, unsettled, artificial mound—though recent excavation has revealed that when in 1138 Henry of Blois, bishop of Winchester, built his new castle at Farnham in Surrey, he caused the mound and the tower keep to be raised together in one build, the one to strengthen the other.

Though some castles of this period lost, therefore, the familiar feature of the motte, and abandoned also the typical 'figure-of-eight' plan of so many early fortresses, the principle and the military philosophy behind them all remained unchanged. The castle still comprised two distinct component parts, the larger enclosure of the bailey, and the citadel, now the keep. Wherever the keep stood within the castle, and whatever its type, shell or tower, square tower or round tower, it was of supreme military importance—a concentrated stronghold for ultimate defence, a castle within a castle. Something of its dominating importance in the contemporary castle can be glimpsed from an aerial photograph of Castle Rising (8), where the great keep of the Albini earls of Sussex stands at bay within the encircling earthworks, and something too from this precept of King John sent to his Justiciar of Ireland, dated August 1204, ordering the building of Dublin castle. 'We command you', it runs, 'that you cause a castle to be raised there ... as strong as possible, with good ditches and strong walls; and build first the keep where afterwards the castle and bailey and other buildings can be conveniently added.'

The keep of the early stone castle, in addition to its military pre-eminence, seems also to have been almost invariably the residence of the lord. Notwithstanding their forbidding external appearance, the residential aspect of the tower keeps is usually apparent within them, however spartan by modern standards they may seem, while the fact that Edward III built new lodgings within the shell at Windsor, and that his son, the Black Prince, held his court within the now ruined lodgings on the mound at Restormel (14), points also to the long continuance of the shell keep's residential rôle. Even so, from the earliest period other residential or non-military buildings, including most often a hall and chapel, were frequently included among the 'houses' in the bailey, for the garrison and serving-men needed accommodation separate from the lord and his family, while a chapel larger than that which the keep

56

could afford was often also regarded as essential. The duplication of accommodation for the lord's family and his servitors or garrison is, naturally enough, a common feature of English castles, found, for example, in the two halls within the thirteenth-century Conway (p. 77) and in many later buildings. But sometimes, even in this period of the keep's supremacy, alternative accommodation was provided in the bailey for the lord himself. This was certainly the case at Windsor where, as we have seen, Henry II built a royal lodging in the upper bailey as well as hall and chambers within the shell keep upon the mound. Indeed the shell keep in particular must always have been as a residence inconvenient no less than secure, and certainly as, in the thirteenth century, the defences of the bailey improved, so there was a tendency to place the principal residential quarters of the castle more spaciously within the safe circuit of its walls.

Inevitably a certain obscurity envelops the internal arrangements of the castle at this early date, just as there is also artificiality in isolating the keep-and-bailey castle as a type, and allotting it arbitrarily to the period of 1150–1250. Some such general summary and chronological arrangement is necessary in the interests of clarity, but it must again be emphasised that the architectural history of the castle is one of continuous development—and also that there were some hundreds of castles each developing upon its own site. And as at the beginning of this chapter the slow transformation in general of the stronghold of earth and timber to the fortress of stone was emphasised, so that transition in particular cases was often gradual and piecemeal. If now it were given to us to ride through the England of, say, A.D. 1200, we should find old and new fortification side by side, here perhaps a tower keep standing within the circuit of stockaded earthworks, and there a stone-built bailey lying at the foot of a mound bearing still its palisade and timber tower. It is chiefly because of this continuous development of the castle, also, that we can no longer see even the completed keep-and-bailey castle as it once appeared. For though much of the great building work of this periode has crumbled away in time, much has been replaced or engulfed by the more sophisticated accumulations of later stonework. Only occasionally, perhaps from aerial photographs of Restormel (14), Castle Rising (8) or of Henry II's keep and inner bailey at Dover (36), can we obtain some impression of what these castles looked like in their original simple strength. Yet, on the other hand, no single feature of them has survived more triumphantly than the square tower keeps, still dominating many an English castle—the classic contribution of the age to medieval military architecture. Crude perhaps but immensely effective, their massive remains can teach some understanding of the English kingdom of their time, 'how it was peopled, and with what sort of men'.

A NOTE UPON THE 'KEEP'

Although in English studies of military architecture the word 'keep' is now generally used and understood, in the Middle Ages it was unknown. To contemporaries the shell keep was generally simply the 'motte' (Latin *mota*) and the tower keep the 'tower' (Latin *turris*) or, later, the 'donjon'. The custom of calling the tower keep simply *'the* tower' has survived of course with our 'Tower of London', where in fact the keep, the White Tower, has given its name to the whole castle. The words 'motte' and 'donjon' have both suffered much change of meaning. The first, in the form of our 'moat', has been shifted from the castle mound to the ditch or fosse which surrounds both the mound and the whole castle. 'Donjon' or 'dungeon', because the tower keep, as difficult to leave as to enter, was sometimes used as a prison, came to be used first, presumably, for the basement of the keep, and subsequently for any subterranean, dark and dismal prison or cell, whether beneath a keep or any other building.

4

The Perfected Castle

THOUGH the art and science of fortification continued to develop and improve in succeeding generations, and some of its developments in some cases were to alter radically the whole concept and design of the castle, the strength of the completed keep-and-bailey castles of the later twelfth and early thirteenth centuries must not be underestimated. They were formidable fortresses and their tower keeps in particular were a near-perfect answer to the resources of contemporary siege-craft. Few English fortresses of this date have survived sufficiently unaltered for us to judge them as they were, but on the Continent the massive remains of Richard I's great creation at Château-Gaillard upon the Seine (p. 64; 19), though it is exceptional in its scale and in some respects looks forward to the great castles of the later thirteenth century, certainly affords a vivid impression of the strength of the best military building of the period. In England at Dover (36), the vast sums spent upon the new work under Henry II and John rivalled even the cost of Château-Gaillard, and the finished result must have been worthy of the epithet, 'the key of the kingdom', which the chronicler Matthew Paris gave it. Other English castles which we know from the evidence of the Pipe Rolls to have been the objects of heavy royal expenditure—the Tower of London, Scarborough, Corfe, Nottingham, Orford, Newcastle upon Tyne, Kenilworth and many more—we may presume to have become by the early thirteenth century first-class fortresses. Kenilworth, to take a case in point, already possessed its massive tower keep long before King John spent the then very large sum of over £1,000 upon the castle. The contemporary chronicler William of Newborough thus describes the royal castle at Nottingham soon after Henry II had completed work there of which the recorded cost is nearly £2,000; 'a castle so strong by nature [i.e. of the site] and by art that, given an adequate garrison, famine alone could overcome it'. These are the king's castles, but that the private baronical castle, even though we have no written evidence of building expenditure for this period, did not lag far if at all behind the royal model, is emphatically shown by surviving archaeological evidence—by the advanced design, for example, of the Bigod walls at Framlingham (16), of the Warenne keep at Conisborough (12), or of the Earl Marshal's keep at Pembroke (13), all raised about the year 1200.

There can be few better testimonies to the very adequate strength and efficiency of the keep-and-bailey castle than the fact that the type continued to be employed throughout the Middle Ages, notwithstanding advances both in the techniques of siege-craft and in the military architecture designed to frustrate them. This continuance, moreover, is not confined only to those castles which, constructed on the keep-and-bailey plan in the twelfth or thirteenth centuries, remained thereafter basically unaltered. Naworth Castle in Cumberland, for example, built by Ralph, Lord Dacre, subsequent to a royal licence granted in 1335, though much rebuilt in the nineteenth century, followed originally the old plan, with a square keep, Dacre Tower, at one corner of a roughly triangular bailey. Etal Castle in Northumberland, raised *c*. 1341–5, also followed the old keep-and-bailey plan (p. 91). A new keep or tower-house was added to Knaresborough by Edward II in 1307–12 at a cost of over £2000, and the remarkable tower-house at Warkworth was built upon the original motte of the ancient castle as late as the last quarter of the same century. The 'pele towers' of the north, whose building in the fourteenth and fifteenth centuries and after we shall have occasion to discuss later (pp. 92–3), were lesser square keeps standing within the small baileys of their walled courtyards. Most remarkable of all, perhaps, is the fact that Edward I's castles in Wales, which taken as a whole represent the triumphant culmination of English military architecture, included among their number, at Flint, a castle designed emphatically on the old keep-and-bailey plan (p. 63).

The typical keep-and-bailey castle of the late twelfth or early thirteenth centuries had, however, its military weaknesses. It was two-piece in design, being made up of two component parts, the keep and the bailey. This duality and the superior strength and importance of the keep therein, often led contemporaries even to distinguish between the keep and the (rest of the) castle. Thus the twelfth-century poet, Jordan Fantosme, in his metrical chronicle of the rebellion of the 'Young King' against his father King Henry II in 1173–4, writes of both Appleby (p. 48) and Carlisle (each of which has a tower keep) as 'the castle and the tower'— *le chastel e la tur*—and official records speak of 'the tower and the castle of Colchester', or 'the castle of Worcester with the motte'. The castle was not integrated, and did not present one co-ordinated and combined defensive system to the field. From the point of view of the attackers, indeed, the castle's defences were one thing after another; first they must take the bailey and then, a sterner task, the keep. Given a determined garrison, this, over and over again, is the pattern of twelfth- and early thirteenth-century sieges as they are described in contemporary accounts; it happened, for example, at Appleby in 1174, at Rochester in 1215, and at Bedford in 1224. Even the elaborate plan of Richard I's beloved Château-Gaillard is designed on traditional principles, presenting one fortified position after another, culminating in the keep, across the line its attackers were forced to follow by the nature of its lofty site (p. 64).

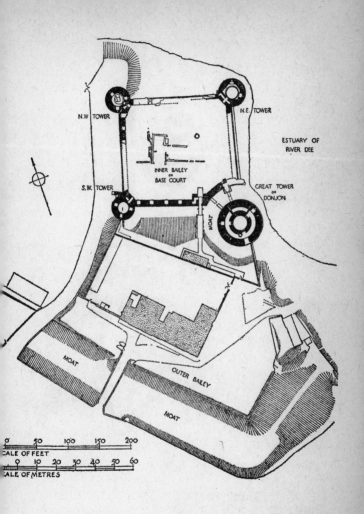

N.W. TOWER

N.E. TOWER

ESTUARY OF
RIVER DEE

INNER BAILEY
OR
BASE COURT

S.W. TOWER

GREAT TOWER
OR
DONJON

MOAT

MOAT

OUTER BAILEY

MOAT

SCALE OF FEET
0   50   100   150   200

SCALE OF METRES
0   10   20   30   40   50   60

Flint, 1277–81: the ground plan

63

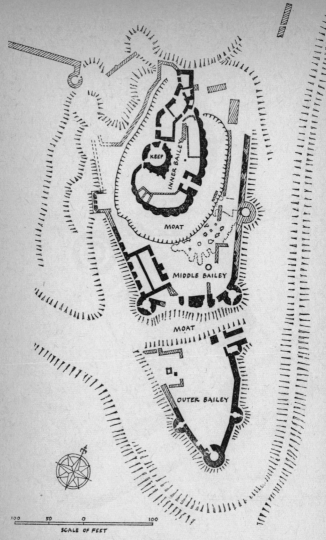

KEEP

INNER BAILEY

MOAT

MIDDLE BAILEY

MOAT

OUTER BAILEY

100   50   0   100
SCALE OF FEET

Château-Gaillard, Les Andelys, *c.* 1197–8 (cf. Figure 19)
*(Redrawn from Malençon's plan, by courtesy
of Monuments Historiques, Paris)*

From the point of view of castle design, the pre-eminent strength and importance of the keep was due chiefly to two causes. First, one ultimate, concentrated strongpoint was a necessity when contemporary methods of fortification were seldom able adequately to defend the whole area of the castle. Secondly, since the keep was generally the principal residence of the lord within the castle, it was the point which he was most concerned to defend. But clearly, however strong and fine the keep, no one would wish to see the rest of his castle overrun if it could be avoided. Even as the defences of the keep were perfected, military engineers were already turning their attention to the bailey, and the eventual perfection of the bailey defences, when and where achieved, rendered the keep redundant and revolutionised the whole concept and design of the castle. These great advances in military architecture made in the thirteenth century were occasioned, as we might expect, by corresponding advances in the means of attack, and they drew inspiration also from the advanced fortification of the Crusaders in the Latin Kingdom of Jerusalem, itself owing something—though neither so much nor so certainly as was at one time thought—to Byzantine fortification inherited from the Roman Empire.

The most important single development in the improvement of the bailey defences was the adoption of the mural or flanking tower. A straightforward wall round the bailey was never an adequate defence. There were obvious limits, including financial, to the thickness with which it could be built, and it was inevitably easier to breach than the close-knit strength of the tower keep, or the wall of the shell keep raised on the lofty eminence of the mound. Above all there was little chance of protecting its outer base once the attackers had succeeded in crossing the ditch to reach it. From an early date castle walls had been provided with battlements, that is to say with crenellations and a rampart walk along the top. By this means the defenders were enabled to fire towards the field while remaining under cover, or to beat off an assault on the summit of the wall by escalade (p. 148), but they could not cover the base of the wall, where the enemy would seek to make a breach with their picks, bores and battering rams, without leaning over and seriously exposing themselves. The answer to the problem, employed by the Romans in their fortifications and descending from them to the Eastern Empire of Byzantium, was the mural or flanking tower. Built at intervals along the wall and projecting outwards from it towards the field, the flanking tower enabled the defenders to cover adequately the outer face and base of the wall while remaining themselves unexposed. In addition to this vital function, the mural towers, by virtue of their superior height, commanded the summit of the wall should the enemy gain it, and also pinned him down there, since, being placed at intervals, they divided the wall into sections. Finally, they were in themselves strongpoints along the circumference of the wall, and, carefully sited, efficiently covered each other.

Though Ludlow can boast certain haphazardly placed mural towers reckoned to date from the closing years of the eleventh century, the wall of Henry II's new inner bailey surrounding his great keep at Dover provides one of the earliest surviving examples of their systematic and scientific employment (36). Henry's work at Dover belongs to the last quarter of the twelfth century, and there is a markedly close resemblance between the mural towers of that royal castle and the thirteen towers systematically employed to defend the enclosure of the inner bailey of earl Roger Bigod's castle of Framlingham (16), rebuilt about the year 1200. In both these early examples the towers are square, and also their projection is entirely outwards, their inner side being flush with the wall, and in most cases left open to the bailey. The advantages of the cylindrical or multi-angular shape, however, which we saw applied to the tower keeps towards the end of the twelfth century, were soon applied to mural towers. In the thirteenth century they reach their finest and final development in the circular drum towers, well displayed at Conway (p.77), Harlech (p. 81) or Beaumaris (p. 78), and are a characteristic feature of English fortification from the later thirteenth century onwards, though the polygonal form was preferred at so fine a castle as Carnarvon (p. 75). The essential feature of the flanking tower was that it should project outwards, and in consequence it was sometimes built as a half-cylinder or polygon, its inner face being more or less flush with the line of the wall. This, we have seen, was done with the towers at Dover and Framlingham and they have their successors at Pembroke or Llanstephan, though the other feature of the earlier towers, that they are left open to the bailey, is very rarely followed in later fortification. The base of the mural tower, like the base of the tower keep, was often splayed out externally for additional strength against attack, and this defence sometimes develops into dramatic batters and spurs such as may be seen at Goodrich (26) or the beaked tower at the north-westerly prow of Dover's outer curtain. Internally the towers were normally divided into two or three storeys, forming a basement and guard-rooms, though they may be worked into the domestic apartments of the castle. The entrance was from the bailey into the basement, and doors on the first storey gave access to the ramparts along the summit of the wall. The use and disposition of the mural towers, and their essential rôle of covering by their flanking fire the outer *enceinte* of the castle, are sufficiently shown, without the need of further comment, by plans and photographs of such thirteenth-century castles as Conway (p. 77; 21), Carnarvon (p. 75; 22), Beaumaris (p. 78; 24) or Flint (p. 63).

In the thirteenth and fourteenth centuries, as in all other centuries of the Middle Ages, particular attention was paid to the fortification of the castle gateway, and it is this period which sees the evolution of those great gatehouses which are such a striking feature of English military architecture, and which lingered on, indeed, beyond the end of the castle's military history as conventional and proud embellishments of thinly defended manor-houses and other buildings. The gateway, once a weak point simply by reason of being an entrance, now becomes the strongest point in the whole circuit of the castle walls, and very often, indeed, the strongest building in the whole castle. As early as the twelfth century the idea of the flanking tower first begins to appear applied to the castle gateway. Thus the entrances to Henry II's new inner bailey at Dover were defended by placing stone towers on either side of the actual gates (36). The impressive gateway at Rockingham, dating in its present form from the reign of Edward I, shows the same method of fortification in its simplest form, save that there the twin towers have become rounded. In these two gateways may be seen the seed from which sprang the fully developed gatehouse of the later thirteenth and fourteenth centuries —at Saltwood (17), Tonbridge, Harlech (p. 81) or Beaumaris (p. 78), to name but a few—all of which are based fundamentally on the plan of twin flanking towers, though above the level of the gateway itself these two towers are now bound together into the one unit of the whole gatehouse. The entrance thus becomes a narrow covered passage, blocked, usually at either end, by a sliding portcullis moving up and down as required in stone grooves. It often also has *meurtrières* or 'murder holes' in the vault above, probably intended to be used as much for the quenching of any fire within the gate as for defence against the persons of assailants. Inside the gatehouse the one essential was a chamber immediately above the entrance passage, in which the portcullis and machicolations could be worked; the rest of the internal space was given over to guardrooms or sometimes to residential apartments.

Because of their massive power, which often makes them the strongest point of the castle and sometimes, as at Dunstanburgh (*c.* 1315), the concentration of almost its entire strength, the great gatehouses have been compared with the tower keeps of earlier castles. The possible similarity seems more marked when we find that some of the finest specimens, at Kidwelly (25), at Harlech or the remarkable northern gatehouse at Beaumaris (24), contain with them sets of residential apartments. Yet though it is true that the idea of one concentrated strongpoint, serving both as the principal defence and the principal residence of the castle, never entirely disappeared from English medieval military architecture, the comparison between the gatehouse and the tower keep must not be pressed too far. The essential function of the gatehouse was to defend the gate, and in so doing it was thrust forward in the face of the enemy instead of standing in reserve as the place of ultimate refuge as the keep usually did. Nor in its aggressive design had it much in common with the solid embodiment of passive defence which characterises the tower keep. Indeed, by virtue of the sweeping advances in fortification which are now our concern, the defence of the whole castle was becoming increasingly an aggressive affair of positive action. And this is nowhere better seen than in the multiplication of gateways and gatehouses themselves, which becomes a marked feature of military architecture from the late thirteenth century onwards. Beaumaris (p. 78), Caerphilly (p. 83), Carnarvon (p. 75) and Conway (p. 77) have two main entrances, eked out in the case of the last three castles by lesser or postern gates. The multiplication of the gateway, reflecting a new confidence in its defence, gave the garrison greater freedom of movement and opportunity to launch sallies or counter-attacks against their assailants, while the enemy was prevented from concentrating his strength at one chosen point by the necessity of closely investing the whole perimeter.

Because the castle gate was so often the point at which the enemy directed his assault, it was frequently provided with an additional fortification in the form of an outer defence or barbican. In its simplest form, as at Warwick or Alnwick, the barbican consists of two parallel walls built out towards the field on either side of the gateway and at right angles to it, thus holding the would-be assailant at arm's length, and forcing him to approach the vital gate itself by a narrow, covered and defended passage-way. Variations on this plan, as before the south gate of the inner bailey at Beaumaris (p. 78), force the assailant to approach at an angle and thus be more exposed to the concentrated fire of the defenders from the gatehouse itself. Elsewhere the barbican becomes an elaborate outwork. The ruins of such an outwork are still plainly to be seen before the gate at Goodrich (26), a very similar and contemporary outwork once existed at the Tower of London, while the barbicans defending the two gates at Conway are almost outer baileys of the main castle enclosure provided with their own flanking towers (p. 77).

The defences of the bailey, so vastly strengthened by the adoption of the flanking tower and the developed gatehouse, were perfected by certain additional details, all again of an aggressive sort. In the thirteenth and fourteenth centuries crenellation remains basically unchanged, but is improved by increasing the number of embrasures in the parapet and correspondingly narrowing the merlons between them. At the same time the merlons were increasingly pierced with firing-loops or slits for the discharge of arrows or bolts from crossbows. This improved crenellation was applied to mural towers and gatehouses no less than to the wall itself. In general, also, the fire-power of the castle was further increased by inserting firing-loops in towers and walls wherever they could be effectively used, and in some cases, as at Carnarvon, Rhuddlan and the Tower, firing-galleries are worked into the walls beneath the line of the battlements. Finally, the crucial defence of the ex-

Rampart and
crenellation

Hoarding

Machicolation

posed outer base of walls and towers was made more efficient by making the battlements in effect overhang it. This was achieved at first by fixing a wooden gallery to the outer summit, accessible from the ramparts, and with apertures in its floor through which missiles could be discharged. A royal writ of December 1240 provides a good example and exposition of such a wooden gallery being fitted to the White Tower at London: at the top of the tower on the south side a gallery is to be made of good strong timber and well leaded over, so that men may see as far as the foot of the tower, and go up and defend it better at need. In process of time this temporary wooden structure, *hurdicia* or hoarding, was sometimes replaced by a stone machicolated overhanging parapet. Such stone machicolation appears as early as the last decade of the twelfth century on Richard I's keep at Château-Gaillard in Normandy, but in England it does not become common until the end of the fourteenth century, and even then is principally confined to gatehouses (17, 18).

The perfection of the bailey defences which was the net result of all these improvements radically altered the whole concept and design of the castle. The new and improved castle of the thirteenth and fourteenth centuries, fully incorporating the new techniques of fortification, was an integrated whole, presenting to an enemy assaulting from any direction a single system of close-knit interrelated defences, in contrast to the two-piece plan and piecemeal defences of the keep-and-bailey castle which preceded it. In form it becomes basically a simple enclosure, either logically quadrangular in plan or exploiting the contours of the ground on which it stands, adequately defended by its towered walls, and no longer needing a keep as one concentrated, ultimate strongpoint to be held should the rest of the castle fall. In consequence, in the greater newly built castles of the period the keep disappears altogether, and in those existing castles, now improved and modernised, falls back into a position of secondary importance. The domestic no less than the military importance of the keep also declines, for the lord of the castle was now able to move down from its lofty but somewhat inconvenient eminence and dwell more comfortably in spacious residential buildings adequately protected by the castle walls. The importance of the mural flanking towers, especially, in thus binding the castle together into a unit can scarcely be overemphasised, while the towers themselves, the multiplication of the gate, the plentiful provision of firing-loops and the development of hoarding and machicolation, all placed the emphasis in defence upon offensive action. In the great castles of the golden age the military rule that attack is the best form of defence finds its embodiment in stone.

Edward I, Edward Longshanks, King of England and Duke

of Aquitaine, has left behind him a popular reputation as the Hammer of the Scots, but his more definite achievement in these islands was the conquest of Wales. To ensure his control of the newly acquired territories, Edward caused eight new castles to be raised, Aberystwyth and Builth in mid-Wales, Beaumaris, Conway, Carnarvon, Flint, Harlech and Rhuddlan in the north. Though both the principles upon which they are raised and many of their features can be found in earlier examples, there is no doubt that the greatest of these Edwardian castles are amongst the finest achievements of medieval military architecture in England, and being built, broadly speaking, in one concentrated operation as new castles upon new sites, with little counting of the cost, they incorporated at the outset and on the grand scale all the advances in fortification made in the thirteenth century which we have been at pains to discuss. These Edwardian castles therefore merit our attention as they challenge our admiration.

Carnarvon (1283–c. 1330) and Conway (1283–7) may be taken together as the two grandest examples in Britain of the new type of castle whose whole united strength was provided by the single circuit of its towered walls (pp. 75, 77; 21, 22). Both, it may be noted, like Aberystwyth, Flint and Rhuddlan among Edward's other Welsh fortresses, were combined with fortified towns, attached to them and built at the same time, though the town defences do not concern us here. Both, in basic design, are simply irregular enclosures adapted to and exploiting the sites on which they stand. A glance at the plans of either provides a vivid lesson in the use and importance of mural towers which contribute so much to the integrated strength of the castle. At Conway drum towers are used, still pleasingly dramatic in the sheer strength of their rotundity, while at Carnarvon the towers are all polygonal in shape. In both there is no point on the *enceinte* of the castle which is not exposed to a withering cross-fire from flanking towers and battlements and a multiplicity of well-placed firing-loops, while medieval fire-power reaches its culmination at the south front of Carnarvon. There two firing-galleries are worked into the walls beneath the level of the crenellated ramparts, each with its loops and embrasures, so that a triple fire can be directed upon an enemy attacking from that direction. Both castles maintain the aggression of their fire-power by having two main gateways, supplemented at Conway by two posterns, and at Carnarvon by three. At Carnarvon both main gates are defended by two great gatehouses; at Conway both main gates lie close between two of the drum towers of the curtain so that no additional gatetowers are necessary, though each is protected by a barbican of sufficient strength and size to be almost an outer ward. Internally both castles were divided originally into two parts by a cross-wall, though both are strong enough to make the precaution seem unnecessary. Lastly, each of these majestic castles, as befitted the residence of princes, originally contained (at Carnarvon they were never entirely completed and have now largely disappeared) a stately series of domestic apartments—hall, chambers, chapel, kitchen—duplicated probably in both cases for the separate use of king and garrison.

More scientifically satisfying even than Conway and Carnarvon in the logical completeness of its design was the concentric castle, the best-known, but by no means the most common, type of late thirteenth- and fourteenth-century fortress. The concentric castle applied the principle of the enclosure adequately fortified by its own towered wall in duplicate. The main enclosure, the inner ward or bailey, which is usually quadrangular in plan, is surrounded by a further wall, often with its own flanking towers, slighter in strength and lower in elevation than the main towered wall which thus covers it by fire-power, and to which it is

74

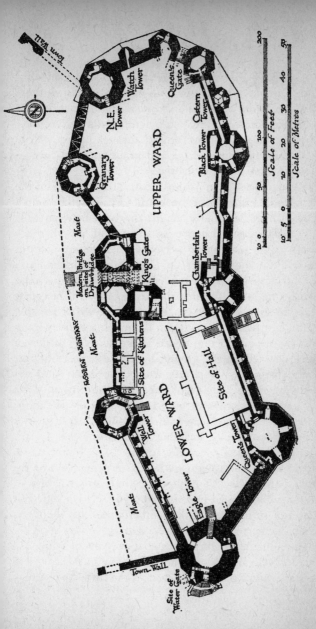

Carnarvon, 1283–c. 1330: ground plan (cf. Figure 22)

simply an outer-ring defence. The outer wall is in effect, if the term be preferred, a vast barbican protecting the whole castle. The space between the inner and outer walls is known as the lists, and is quite narrow at least in those castles built from their foundation on the concentric pattern. It was sometimes divided by cross-walls into sections, so that an enemy, having broken through the outer defences, could be pinned down and in his enforced concentration be more easily destroyed.

Edward I's castles in Wales, again, provide some of the most splendid examples of concentric fortresses to be found. Amongst them Beaumaris (p. 78; 24) built between 1295 and *c*. 1330 is beyond doubt the finest, and 'no other Edwardian castle presents so perfectly scientific a system of defence' (Hamilton Thompson). Logically quadrangular in plan, the castle consists of two symmetrical enclosing walls, of which the inner, forming the castle proper, is of course by far the stronger. Both make the utmost use of flanking towers, the narrow lists between them being entirely dominated by the great drum towers and gatetowers of the inner ward. Sited on flat ground by the sea, the castle was entirely surrounded by a wet moat. The inner ward has two entrances opposite each other on its north and south sides respectively, each defended by a majestic gatehouse. The northern gatehouse contained within its ample interior residential apartments, including an imposing hall, for the king or his resident constable. In the defence of its gates, as in so many of its features, Beaumaris can stand as the culmination of English medieval military architecture. In addition to their own immense strength, supplemented by a barbican in the case of the southern, and the additional covering defence given to each by flanking towers on either side, both main gatehouses have their corresponding entrances to the outer ward built out of line to them, so that an enemy carrying these first gates of the castle and gaining

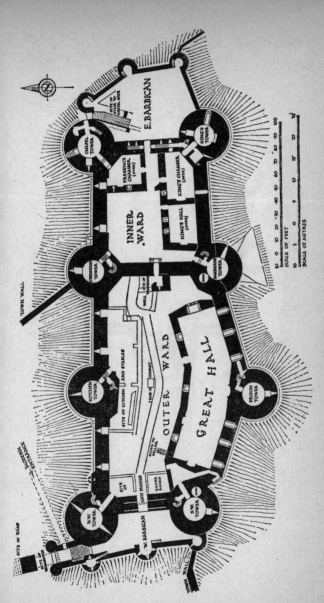

Conway, Carnarvonshire, 1283–7: ground plan (cf. Figure 21)

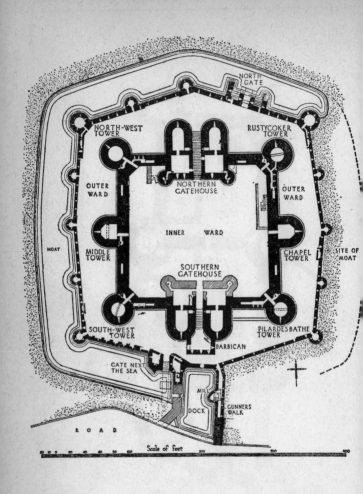

Beaumaris, Anglesey, c. 1295–c. 1330: ground plan (cf. Figure 24)

Within the plan, the following labels appear:

NORTH GATE

NORTH-WEST TOWER

RUSTYCOKER TOWER

OUTER WARD

NORTHERN GATEHOUSE

OUTER WARD

INNER WARD

MIDDLE TOWER

CHAPEL TOWER

MOAT

SOUTHERN GATEHOUSE

SITE OF MOAT

SOUTH-WEST TOWER

PILARDESBATHE TOWER

BARBICAN

GATE NEXT THE SEA

MILL DOCK

GUNNERS WALK

R O A D

Scale of feet

the lists is forced to approach the main gates at an angle, and expose his flank to the raking fire of the defenders.

Two further excellent examples of the concentric fortress are included among the Edwardian castles in Wales. Harlech in Merioneth (p. 81; 23), raised between 1283 and 1290, rivals Beaumaris in the military precision of its design, though here its builders were aided in the task of fortification by the lofty eminence of the rocky site they chose. If we discount some minor and rather straggling outer works down the rock to north and west, which formed no part of the defences proper, the castle itself is roughly quadrangular in plan, the walls of the inner ward having four boldly projecting, cylindrical flanking towers, one at each corner. There is only one main gateway to the inner ward, defended by a great gatehouse very similar to the gatehouses at Beaumaris, and containing, like its northern counterpart there, a set of residential apartments. It is set on the eastern side of the castle, facing and aggressively defending the least inaccessible approach. There is no second main gateway at Harlech, probably because the elevated site rendered it impracticable, and probably for the same reason no elaborate series of flanking towers was thought necessary for the defence of the outer ward. The narrow lists between the inner and outer walls appear to be divided at least at one point by a cross-wall, and in the inner ward the residential apartments, other than those within the gatehouse, are logically and neatly ranged along, and sheltered by, the walls. The defences of the castle were completed by a wide moat on the south and east sides, and on the north and west by the precipitous descent of the rock on which it stood. Lastly, Rhuddlan in Flintshire (p. 82), built between 1277 and 1882, and one of the earliest of Edward I's castles in Wales, is 'a simple but perfect concentric castle' (Douglas Simpson). Again it follows the logical quadrangular plan, and here the walls of the inner ward are strengthened by flanking towers at the four corners only—a single drum tower at the north and south corners, and at the east and west corners twin drum towers defending the two main gateways set diagonally opposite each other. Again the wall of the outer bailey has no series of flanking towers, and the whole castle is surrounded by a wide moat on the three sides where the ground permits.

Though the greatest of the royal Edwardian castles in Wales stand grandly among the supreme achievements of English medieval military architecture, it is interesting, and important to the proper understanding of medieval society and politics, to notice that in both majesty and strength they are closely rivalled by some at least of the contemporary castles of the king's subjects. Here pride of place goes at once to Caerphilly in Glamorgan (p. 83; 20), the fortress of the greatest subject of the Crown, the Clare earl of Hertford and Gloucester. Perhaps the finest of the castles as it is the largest in overall extent, antedating the Edwardian castles which it may well have served to inspire, Caerphilly added to its core of a powerful quadrangular concentric fortress a most extensive system of water defences, barbicans and outworks, and had one of the most elaborately defended approaches in all Britain. Kidwelly (25), too, in Carmathenshire, may be cited among the most powerful baronial fortresses. The stronghold of the family of de Chaworth, built in the form in which it now stands in the late thirteenth and early fourteenth centuries, it is, if we exclude its outworks to north and south, a concentric castle with a difference. The inner ward is quadrangular, with four massive drum towers, one at each corner. It is protected on three sides by the wall of the crescent-shaped outer ward, with its own flanking towers and an enormous gatehouse at its southern extremity, which, like the gatehouses at Harlech and Beaumaris, contains a hall and other domestic apartments. The fourth side of the inner ward

16 Framlingham, Suffolk (c. 1200) : the castle of the Bigod earls of Norfolk. An early example of the use of flanking towers

18 (above) Carisbrooke, Isle of Wight: the gatehouse (1380)

17 (left) Saltwood, Kent: the gatehouse (c. 1383)

19 Château-Gaillard, Les Andelys (1197–8): the castle of Richard I which guards the Seine approach to Normandy (cf. p. 64)

20   Caerphilly, Glamorgan: the stronghold of the Clare earls of Hertford and Gloucester; a splendid concentric castle of the later thirteenth century, with elaborate outworks and water defences (cf. p. 93).

21 Conway, Carnarvonshire (1283–7) (cf. p. 77)

22. CONWAY NP (1283 × 1330), from the south (cf. p. 75)

23 Harlech, Merionethshire (1283–90) (cf. p. 81)

24 Beaumaris, Anglesey (1295–c. 1330): a perfect example of a concentric castle (cf. p. 78)

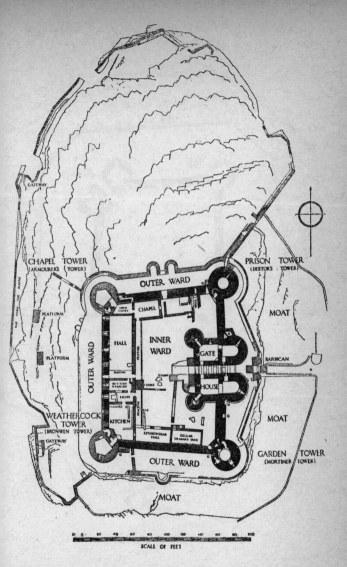

Harlech, Merionethshire, 1283–90: ground plan (cf. Figure 23)

6 English Medieval Castles

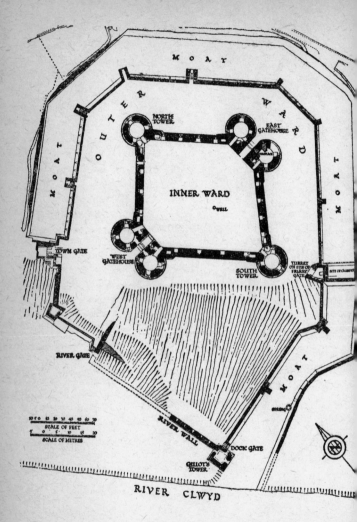

MOAT

OUTER WARD

WARD

MOAT

MOAT

NORTH
TOWER

EAST
GATEHOUSE

INNER WARD

○WELL

TOWN GATE

WEST
GATEHOUSE

SOUTH
TOWER

THREE
ON SITE OF
FRIARS GATE

SITE OF CHAMBER

RIVER GATE

SCALE OF FEET
SCALE OF METRES

MOAT

SPRING

RIVER WALL

DOCK GATE

GILLOT'S
TOWER

RIVER CLWYD

Rhuddlan, Flintshire, 1277–82: ground plan

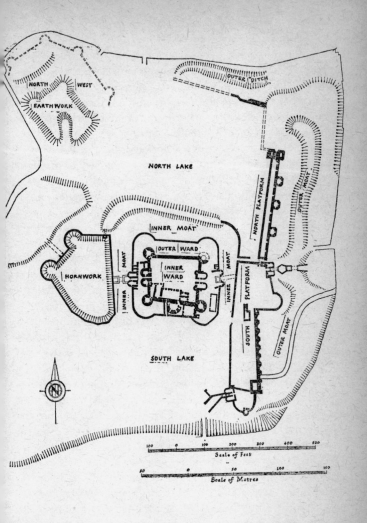

Caerphilly, Glamorgan: ground plan (cf. Figure 20)

needs no further protection than the river Gwendraeth Fach, upon whose steep bank it stands.

It must be stressed, however, that all the great castles of the late thirteenth and early fourteenth centuries which we have so far examined, Conway and Carnarvon, Beaumaris, Harlech and Rhuddlan, Caerphilly and Kidwelly, built at the outset to the new designs and incorporating all the improvements of fortification developed principally in the course of the thirteenth century, are themselves exceptional. They are partly exceptional, first, in the scale of their magnificence. They are all in Wales, where throughout most of the Middle Ages a more or less chronic state of wars and rumours of wars between the Marcher barons and the Welsh, and occasionally between the Marcher barons themselves, called forth all that was best in military architecture, while the castles of King Edward I in particular were built with the specific purpose of holding down newly conquered territory. Yet not all even of the royal Edwardian fortresses in Wales were built on the scale of a Conway, a Carnarwon or a Beaumaris. Flint (p. 63), for example, was constructed on an overall plan reminiscent of the keep-and-bailey castle, though it makes the fullest use of flanking towers and its great donjon is thrust forward to command the outer bailey and the harbour. But chiefly the seven castles described are exceptional simple because they were new. Though Carnarvon and Kidwelly stand at least partially upon sites previously fortified, and though the building of Carnarvon and Beaumaris was carried out in several instalments spread over some forty years, they were all of them, broadly speaking, new works raised from their foundations in one period and in one overall, more or less concentrated operation. In this they stand in sharp distinction to the normal castle whose architectural history is one of an early origin followed by a gradual and continuous process of growth and development over the centuries.

84

In the thirteenth and fourteenth centuries, as in all periods of the Middle Ages subsequent to the first century of Norman establishment, fortification and castle-building more commonly took the form of the strengthening and improvement of existing castles in accordance with changing needs and techniques. Sometimes, where this was done on a grand scale, the final result almost matched a Beaumaris in the scientific complexity of concentric fortification. Thus the Tower of London (27), in the course of the thirteenth century, became one of the largest concentric fortresses in the country by the rebuilding and building of the walls of the middle and outer baileys, the cylindrical flanking towers of the former dominating the narrow outer ward or lists, a broad ditch surrounding the whole, and the main entrance defended by a barbican and a series of characteristic gatehouses, of which the Middle Tower and the Byward Tower remain. Here it is particularly interesting to see that, as the result of these encircling developments, the great square keep, the White Tower, which in the eleventh century must have been almost the entire strength of the castle, is reduced to comparative military insignificance, though visually it still dominates the whole to which it gives its name. At Dover (36) similar development, begun by Henry II himself and continued by his successors in the thirteenth century, produced another large, though less regular, concentric fortress, the great keep and inner bailey being surrounded and flanked by the sweeping outer curtain, with its long series of mural towers, and the striking and powerful Constable's Gate built to replace King John's gateway at the north-west of the fortress after the experience of the siege of 1216.

Elsewhere major building works took the form of enlargement by the addition of new baileys, their walls incorporating flanking towers and aggressive gatehouses according to the new principles, even though the site did not

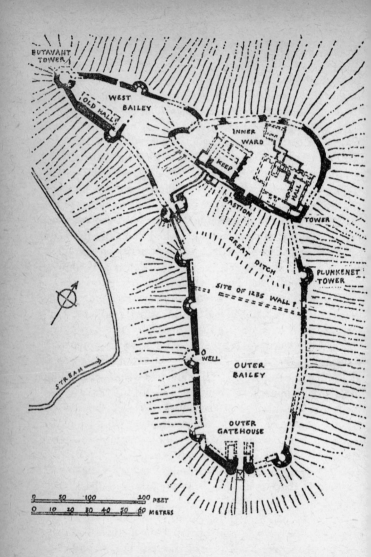

Corfe, Dorset: the ground plan

lend itself to the concentric development. Thus the Dorset fortress of Corfe (p. 86), whose keep and inner bailey, the core of the castle, date from the earlier twelfth century, and whose once fine series of domestic buildings within the inner bailey date from the reign of John, received the curtain walls of its middle bailey to the west and its outer bailey to the south and east in the thirteenth century. Both incorporate the now essential flanking towers, of which the most notable are the polygonal 'Butavant' Tower at the apex of the middle bailey and the fine series of half-cylindrical towers along the more exposed western side of the outer bailey. This outer bailey still contains, also, at its southern extremity, the substantial remains of a gatehouse, built on the usual plan of twin flanking towers one on either side of the entrance passage. At Chepstow, in Monmouthshire, a new bailey was added at either end of the original castle enclosure on its elongated, elevated site above the river Wye, both of them embellished and defended by drum towers and gatehouses. The larger of these new courts, to the east, included an elaborate series of residential apartments built against the least exposed wall above the river, while it is especially noteworthy that here at Chepstow a significant accompaniment of these thirteenth-century developments was the conversion of the original keep in the centre of the castle to provide more sumptuous and spacious accommodation. Elsewhere existing castles were bound together into one simple, integrated unit by the complete building or rebuilding of their bailey defences. Thus Goodrich (26) became, in the late thirteenth and fourteenth centuries, a typical and satisfying fortress of the period, logically quadrangular in plan, with a drum tower at each of three angles and a strong gatehouse at the fourth, the whole surrounded on two sides by a moat and on two sides by an outer line of stonework, with a half-moon barbican in front of the gate. And in the centre of this imposing self-sufficient structure, the twelfth-century square tower keep remained (and still remains), though rendered militarily almost unnecessary by the lofty walls and towers which surrounded it. At far-off Middleham in Yorkshire, the northern seat of the great house of Neville, precisely the same development took place, and the enormous twelfth-century rectangular tower keep is engulfed by the later walls and towers of the quadrangular castle enclosure.

At many other castles the developments of the period were piecemeal only: the addition of flanking towers, like the Gray Mare's Tail at Warkworth, to weaker or more exposed sections of the curtain; the provision upon an existing *enceinte* of a new gatehouse as at Trematon; and, almost invariably, the improvement and rebuilding of domestic apartments to gain the more spacious living which the new strength of castle walls made possible. Inevitably such piecemeal additions and slow development meant the survival of ancient building and old forms. Keeps, tower and shell, continued in use, either still fulfilling their pristine rôle as the ultimate strongpoint of the fortress, or reduced to secondary importance by new walls and towers about them. Many castles, and amongst them some of the most important, still retained the original layout of their Norman motte-and-bailey earthwork, though long since built in stone and the circuit of their walls now greatly strengthened by flanking towers and gatehouses. Nor was this conservatism confined to the maintenance of existing buildings. It was in this period that the tower keeps of York (15) and Pontefract were built, each of them advanced and unusual in plan, but each of them standing upon a motte, and reminding us that the development of military architecture in this country did not follow at all times and in all places that steady line of progression which summarised accounts imply.

5

The Decline of the Castle

THE period under review in the last chapter, roughly (since all 'periods' of castle architecture are arbitrary and overlap) the century from 1250 to 1350, represents the Golden Age of English medieval military architecture, and after it the remaining architectural history of the castle is one of rather saddening anti-climax. The greatest new castles of that age, Conway and Carnarvon, Beaumaris and Harlech, Caerphilly and Kidwelly, were never surpassed in the years to come, and had indeed no rivals and few successors. Little advance save in detail was made from the principles of fortification worked out in the thirteenth century, of which they had been the supreme exposition, and which had also been applied piece-meal to an hundred-and-one fortresses throughout the land, then strengthened and improved. The techniques of military architecture, if they did not remain entirely stationary, were applied more and more diffusely and eventually less and less frequently. Generally speaking, from the latter half of the fourteenth century, though somewhat more tardily in the far north and in Wales, the military importance of the castle began to decline. The complex reasons for this decline we shall have occasion to discuss later, towards the end of this book (pp. 193–6); here it is enough to say that it results principally from the changing political condition of the kingdom on the one hand and the changing character of warfare on the other. Not even the upheaval of the Wars of the Roses, though here and there partly responsible for new fortification, caused any significant revival of castle-building on the old scale, for warfare by then turned less upon the castle and had become more a matter of battles in the open field. Finally, we must emphasise here that the importance of one particular reason commonly given for the military decline of the castle, namely the introduction of gunpowder into warfare, must not be exaggerated. The adoption of gunpowder in this country was slow, and by the time that ordnance of sufficient power seriously to threaten contemporary fortification was at all common, the decline of the castle was already advanced. Gunpowder was no more than one of many other and deeper causes for the loss of the castle's military importance, and its own direct effects upon castle architecture, which is here our concern, were in this country slight.

The unique feature of the castle from the beginning had been that it was both a residence and a fortress. The decline in its military importance, therefore, resulted architecturally in an increasing concentration upon its domestic amenities at the expense or to the neglect of its defences, until, passing through the phase of the fortified manor-house, we reach the country house of late Tudor and Elizabethan times, with perhaps only a moat to remind us of its militant antecedents, and the castle properly so called ceases to exist as a living architectural form. Such, in broad outline, is the remaining architectural history of the castle during a period roughly defined as extending from 1350 to 1550. The process, however, is long and gradual and studded with exceptions.

The far north of England, towards Scotland, provides the most extensive exception to the general decline of the military importance of the castle in the fourteenth and fifteenth centuries. There the endemic local warfare immortalised in the 'Border Ballads', the continuous threat and frequent occurrence of Scottish raids—themselves the reaction to what Douglas Simpson calls the 'unhappy venture' of Edward I's attack upon Scotland—necessitated the increase rather than the decline of serious fortification. For this localised warfare followed the familiar pattern of raids and counter-raids by comparatively small forces, to which the castle or fortified house was a more or less sufficient answer. The new castles of the fourteenth and later centuries in the far north cannot, for the most part, be numbered among the great fortresses of the realm. They do not, like the Edwardian castles in Wales, represent a major military operation by the Crown for the defence or expansion of the realm. Indeed the great fortresses of the north had been long since founded—at Newcastle and Carlisle, Bamburgh, Alnwick, Durham and elsewhere—and much of the new fortification of this later period represents rather the minor works of lesser landlords, constrained by the new circumstances of virulent Scottish incursions to defend themselves as best they could. Bywell in Northumberland, built about 1430, it is true, is the work of the great Neville family, and, though not perhaps a fortress of the first rank, embodies some of the most advanced principles of contemporary fortification in aggressively concentrating its main strength in a powerful and well-machicolated gatehouse. Elsewhere, northern fortification in the later Middle Ages shows a remarkable conservatism. Etal in Northumberland, for example, which took its present form subsequent to a royal licence granted to Robert Manners in 1341, is essentially a lesser keep-and-bailey castle after the twelfth-century manner, with a rectangular tower keep standing half in and half out of a simple bailey, the latter embellished only with a rectangular gatehouse in the corner opposite the keep and a small square tower in its southwest angle. Naworth in Cumberland, built about the same time, followed originally the same plan, and Edlingham in Northumberland (*c.* 1350) consists merely of a simple, walled, rectangular enclosure with a square keep at one end and perhaps a gatehouse at the other.

In fact it is very difficult to distinguish at all clearly between these lesser castles and the 'pele towers', dating from the fourteenth and fifteenth centuries and later, which are such a well-known and characteristic feature of the far north. The pele tower was simply a rectangular tower, the residence of its owner, standing within a 'barmkin' or simple, small, walled courtyard which lacked all elaborate niceties of flanking tower or gatehouse, and was used chiefly for the protection of animals and crops from marauders. The towers themselves vary in size and elaboration from the almost insignificant proportions and extreme simplicity of the Vicar's Pele at Corbridge to the more imposing structures at Chipchase (29) and Belsay, with their turrets and elaborately crenellated and machicolated parapets. The internal arrangements commonly comprise three storeys, the lowest being a storage basement and the two upper storeys being residential. Each floor usually consists of one large apartment with or vithout lesser chambers. Some of the larger towers, like Chipchase, have a small projecting wing, giving to the whole a truncated L-shaped plan, and containing small chambers, the entrance and a staircase. Elsewhere the stairs were commonly in an angle of the tower, and the entrance, like that of tower keeps, is often at first-storey level.

It is clear that the pele towers were simplified and usually smaller rectangular keeps, just as the combination of pele tower and barmkin was a much simplified version of the twelfth-century keep-and-bailey castle, and it is perhaps unfortunate and confusing that the fact should be obscured by the use of different terminology. That these pele towers and barmkins of the fourteenth and fifteenth centuries should have been built upon so old a pattern is not so much due to the conservatism of the north—though conservatism is at times a feature of northern military architecture in the later Middle Ages—as to the brute facts of the situation which produced them. They were raised all over the northern counties (and on the other side of the border in southern Scotland) by lesser gentry who had not hitherto felt the need to live in castles, to meet the new conditions of increased border warfare and insecurity. For them the large, elaborate and vastly expensive structure of a major castle, built in accordance with the most advanced principles of fortification, was quite out of the question, and scarcely necessary for the type of small-scale warfare in which they were involved. The most obvious, simplest and least expensive form of fortified dwelling, on the other hand, was the rectangular tower-house, and by the addition of a courtyard enclosed with a stout wall a man might hope to protect not only his person and family but also his chattels from the depredations of 'the King's enemies, the Scots'.

As opposed to these minor works in the far north, the Welsh borderlands, where also to some extent the continued possibility of local warfare urged the continuance of serious fortification, produced, at Raglan in Monmouthshire (95), one more example of a castle on the grand scale, a century after the completion of the great Edwardian Welsh fortresses. Though Raglan was still undergoing improvements as late as the seventeenth century, the castle as it now stands is mainly the work of Sir William ap Thomas, 'The Blue Knight of Gwent', and Sir William Herbert, later earl of Pembroke, his son, in the fifteenth century. In form it is an irregular enclosure strengthened by powerful mural towers, with two gateways of which the principal one is built on the familiar plan of a pair of elongated flanking towers one on either side of the entrance. Both this gatehouse and the adjacent mural tower are heavily machicolated in stone, and provide an excellent example of this particular advance in the details of fortification in the later Middle Ages. Inside, the main enclosure of the castle is divided into two by the central range of domestic buildings which includes the great hall—an arrangement which, significantly enough, enabled these buildings to be both more spacious and better lighted than the earlier custom of building them against the inner face of the bailey wall. But at Raglan they remain secure, and the castle shows little of that lowering of the guard which is typical of so many of its contemporaries. The most notable feature of the whole work is the Yellow Tower of Gwent, an immensely strong and self-sufficient hexagonal donjon or tower-house, standing surrounded by its own moat, and almost entirely separate from the main structure, with which it was originally connected only by a narrow, well-defended stone causeway. Though this remarkable building, standing in advance of and midway between the two gates, aggressively defends the main approach, it is yet reminiscent of the tower keeps of old, and is a notable feature of a fortress which one would have thought perfectly capable of defending itself without the addition of such a detached citadel.

Though in the main body of England the period 1350 to 1550 saw, from the broad view, the increasing domestication of the castle, the late fourteenth century produced a number of castles fully and comprehensively fortified. Amongst them we may note Nunney in Somerset, built about 1375 and remarkable in following the old keep-and-bailey plan. The bailey has now almost entirely disappeared but seems to have had only the simplest defences. Almost the entire strength of the castle was concentrated in the keep or tower-house, a lofty structure of very advanced design, comprising an oblong body with a cylindrical tower at each corner, the whole heavily machicolated. In contrast to the conservative overall plan of Nunney, the design of Queenborough Castle on the Isle of Sheppey in Kent, begun in 1361, was so advanced as to be unique in this coun-

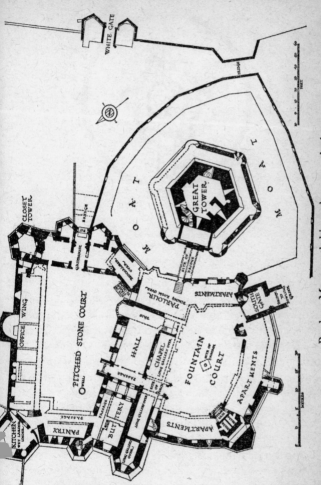

Raglan, Monmouthshire: the ground plan

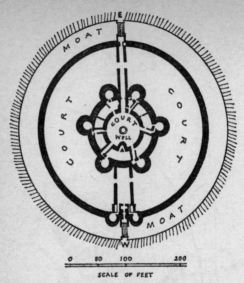

Queenborough, Isle of Sheppey, Kent, 1361–77

try. The castle was destroyed by Parliament in the seventeenth century but surviving drawings show it to have been both perfectly circular and perfectly concentric. The outer *enceinte* was a strong, plain circular wall, surrounded by a moat with a main gate defended by twin towers on the west, and a postern directly opposite on the east. The loftier wall of the inner bailey was defended by six cylindrical towers, two of which were placed close together on the east to form the main entrance. The residential buildings of the castle were ranged round the wall of the inner bailey, leaving a circular courtyard in the centre. Devices which have all the simplicity of genius added to the strength of the castle. Open walled passage-ways connected the outer gates to the inner bailey, and thus pinned down an enemy who should carry those gates and affordered the garrison a last chance of driving him back. At the same time the walled passage-ways divided and blocked the outer bailey after the common fashion of concentric castles. Lastly, it can be seen that the gateway of the inner bailey is placed as far away as possible from the main outer gateway. If, therefore, the latter should fall and the enemy gain the outer bailey, he is forced to move half-way round its circumference, exposed all the way to the fire-power of the inner walls, to reach the entrance of the inner bailey from which he is still cut off by its passage walls. Queenborough was a royal castle, commissioned by Edward III both to guard the coast against the threat of French invasion and as a residence for himself. It was built between 1361 and 1377 and cost, together with the unfortified town and port founded with it, over £25,000. The master mason responsible for the work was not, as is sometimes stated, Henry Yevele, but an older and then more distinguished mason called John Box, who had previously served the king at Calais and Westminster Palace.

More typical of its period than either Nunney or Queenborough, is Bolton in Wensleydale, Yorkshire, raised by Sir Richard le Scrope, the Lord Chancellor, subsequent to a royal licence granted him in 1379. The castle is a compact, quadrangular structure, with lofty walls flanked and over-topped by four massive rectangular towers, placed one at each corner, and two lesser rectangular towers, one in the centre of each longer side. There is no separate gatehouse, but the main entrance, being placed alongside the south-east angle tower, was sufficiently defended by it. The particularly noteworthy feature of this powerful castle is that its domestic buildings, which include the usual great hall and chapel, are neatly and conveniently disposed round all four sides, incorporating the towers, and leaving an open courtyard in the centre. Moreover, these domestic buildings are not, as was commonly the case in earlier castles, merely built up against the sheltering outer walls, but are built of a piece with them, and form part and parcel of the compact whole.

The same logical, quadrangular plan was followed in two other contemporary northern castles, at Sheriff Hutton, also in Yorkshire, built by John de Neville in *c.* 1382 and now much ruined, and at the much-altered and still-inhabited Lumley in County Durham, first built by Sir Ralph Lumley in *c.* 1389. It was also followed in the south, with more advanced features and greater strength, at Bodiam in Sussex (28; p. 99). Bodiam, like Queenborough, was intended to guard the coast against French invasion during the Hundred Years War, and the licence issued in October 1385 to its founder, Sir Edward Dalyngrigge, empowers him 'to make a castle ... in defence of the adjacent country against the king's enemies'. Again the castle combines in one solid quadrangular unit both residential buildings and defences, but here the angle towers are in the form of boldly projecting cylinders in contrast to the conservatively square towers of the northern castles. Also a fine gatehouse occupies the centre of the north face and a lesser postern gatetower stands opposite on the south, both heavily machicolated. In the centre of each remaining side, to east and west, stands a rectangular tower. The whole castle is surrounded by a broad lake, and the main entrance was originally elaborately defended not only by its gatehouse but also by an enforced right-angled approach, comprising an outwork, barbican and two drawbridges.

Though not to be compared in sheer power and size with, for example, the Edwardian castles in Wales, in many respects these quadrangular castles of the late fourteenth century can be regarded as the last and most logically satisfying development of the castle proper, combining to perfection its twin rôles of residence and fortress. Especially,

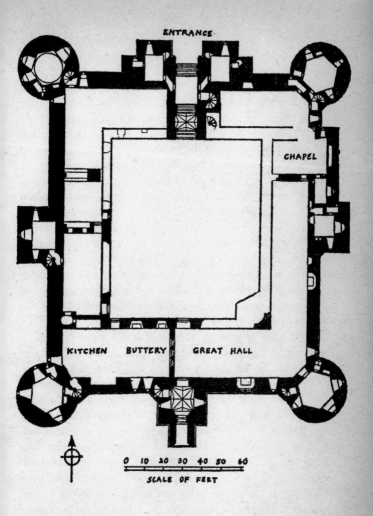

ENTRANCE

CHAPEL

KITCHEN BUTTERY GREAT HALL

0 10 20 30 40 50 60
SCALE OF FEET

Bodiam, Sussex, *c.* 1385: the ground plan (cf. Figure 28)

perhaps, is this true of Bodiam, whose uncompromising
strength yet promised good living within, while the whole
structure, set in its broad lake, is touched with a rare
beauty absent from the grimmer, more grandiose fortresses,
Conway, Caerphilly or Harlech, founded a century before.
In these late quadrangular castles also—Bodiam, Bolton,
Sheriff Hutton, Lumley— the residential buildings become
for the first time an integral part of the whole, as opposed
to miscellaneous structures placed here and there within
the bailey. Moreover, built as a continuous range round
four sides of a quadrangle, they could contain not only the
communal hall, chapel, kitchens, guardrooms and the like,
but also a greater number of more conveniently disposed
private chambers which changing social standards now
required. This development is important because, though
in the four castles we have noticed residential comfort does
not take priority over considerations of defence, elsewhere
from the late fourteenth century onwards, as the military
importance of the castle declines, so castle-building shows
an increasing concentration on domestic amenities at the
expense of fortification.

The change is seen at once, and is the more striking in
occurring so far north, at Raby in County Durham. Raby,
built mainly in the last quarter of the fourteenth century,
was no secondary work of a minor lord but the seat of the
princely Neville family. Yet, though a curtain wall embellished with a strong gatehouse is thrown round it like a
loose girdle, and though the main pile has in places masonry of immense thickness and incorporates some four
strong towers, the place is emphatically first and foremost
a residence, to which certain piecemeal defences have been
added. Its ground plan has a spacious, comfortable, almost
haphazard untidiness which could never have been tole-
rated in a building designed to face a serious and full-scale
attack. The transition of the castle from a fortress in which

one lives to a residence which one may, perhaps, have to defend, is even more clearly seen at Wingfield in Derbyshire, built in the middle of the fifteenth century. Here the site is naturally strong, the buildings are disposed in orderly fashion round two courtyards each with a defended gateway, and the main walls are of strong width and good stone. Yet the beautiful range of ruined domestic buildings which are the most striking feature, the well-lighted hall with its surviving traceried bay window, the absence of any series of flanking towers to bind the whole together, and indeed the absence of any serious military feature save one strong tower in the south-west corner of the upper court, all give the lie to any serious military purpose. 'The primary object of the house at Wingfield was to give comfort and pleasure; and its type is as far removed from the military perfection of Caerphilly or Harlech as it can possibly be' (Hamilton Thompson).

Wingfield in Derbyshire, a product of the troubled reign of Henry VI, is a splendid example of a late-medieval fortified manor-house, and, though outstanding in its erstwhile magnificence and fine workmanship, it is typical of its age. For with the late fourteenth and fifteenth centuries strong and comprehensively fortified castles become the exception so far as new works are concerned, and we enter the era of the fortified manor, the half-way house between the castle proper and the undefended country mansion of Elizabethan and subsequent periods. It must be emphasised that the type of building itself is not new. The castle was always a residence, and in the last resort it was the degree of fortification which earned the proud title of castle and distinguished it from the purely civil dwelling. At all periods of the Middle Ages there were buildings, as difficult for contemporaries as for us to classify, which stood somewhere between the two extremes. Domesday Book itself, compiled only some twenty years after the coming of the

Normans, speaks of *domus defensabiles,* i.e. 'defensible houses'. At Little Wenham in Suffolk (31) there still stands, in perfect and inhabited preservation, a very pleasing thirteenth-century example of such a defensible house, in form something between a small rectangular tower keep and such a contemporary civil hall as that at Boothby Pagnell in Lincolnshire (p. 40), while at Markenfield in Yorkshire a very similar little tower-house of comparable date still retains its bailey or enclosure of stone-built farm buildings and other appurtenances, its gatehouse and its moat. Another and better-known example of a small defensible manor-house of the thirteenth century still stands at Stokesay in Shropshire (32), fortified in its present form with a strong keep-like tower at the southern end of the hall by Laurence de Ludlow about the year 1291. Acton Burnell in Shropshire is another pleasing example of an early fortified manor-house, roughly contemporary with Stokesay. But as the military need for the full-scale defences of the castle proper declined from the later fourteenth century onwards, the fortified manor-house ceased to be, as it were, the *pis aller* for those who could afford, or hoped they needed, nothing better, and became the normal residence of the great.

Not all the fortified manor-houses of the later fourteenth and fifteenth centuries were entirely new buildings. The perfection of the techniques of fortification by this time, together with the declining necessity for the residences of the great to take the form of fully defensive castles, made the addition of piecemeal defences to an existing manor-house, after the manner of Stokesay, both easier and more common. 'Licences to crenellate' existing houses (46) are numerous under Edward III, Richard II and their successors, and though the finished result was sometimes a castle as at Bodiam or Allington (47), they produced with increasing frequency fortified manor-houses incorporating a greater or lesser amount of new building. The plan of the fortified manor naturally varied. At Old Wardour in Wiltshire, raised in the 1390s the old keep-and-bailey layout still unmistakably lingers, though the low and not noticeably strong wall round the bailey, and the emphatically civilian windows of the great tower-house within the bailey, both deny its claim to be considered as a serious castle. Sometimes, again, as at the majestic pile of Haddon Hall in Derbyshire and Thornbury in Gloucestershire, the latter begun as late as 1511, the two-court plan of Wingfield is followed. But perhaps most common of all was the compact and convenient quadrangular plan, very often surrounded with a wet moat. This we saw also to be the last logical development of the completely defensible fortress, and in it we can follow, indeed, the gradual decline of the castle as a military building, and the slow elimination of defensive features from the dwellings of the great. Thus the plan of Bodiam is found, but with varying degree of declining strength, at the slightly earlier Maxstoke in Warwickshire (*c.* 1345), at Shirburn in Oxfordshire (*c.* 1380), at Wingfield in Suffolk (*c.* 1384), at Herstmonceux in Sussex (33) (*c.* 1440), at Hever in Kent (*c.* 1462), at the uncompleted Kirby Muxloe in Leicestershire (43) (*c.* 1480), and at Oxburgh Hall in Norfolk (*c.* 1480). In the last of these (34), built in brick, the angle towers of the earlier examples are no longer found, the plentiful windows are open to the world, ornamental chimneys pierce the skyline above the scarcely less ornamental battlements, and the great gatehouse and the moat are almost the only remaining defensive features. From Oxburgh Hall it is but a short step to the purely residential Tudor country houses, some of which retained the quadrangular form, like Castle Ashby in Northamptonshire (begun in the reign of Elizabeth I and completed as late as 1624), and some, like Playford and Helmingham in Suffolk of many, retained the moat.

103

Whatever their form, the fortified manor-houses have to the modern beholder a peculiar beauty of their own and, withal, an air of peace which is not entirely the result of the passage of time. For in their building architects and those who commissioned them were increasingly⁻ released from the stern necessities of defence, and enabled to concentrate on domestic comfort and dignity with an eye also to aesthetic appearance. We may notice, however, that the gatehouse, which for so long had received the most careful attention of castle designers, commonly remains, as at Kirby Muxloe (43) or Hever, the strongest military feature of the fortified manor. Yet at Oxburgh the towering, seven-storeyed gatehouse (34) has a somewhat bogus air, and one suspects that in practice its serious defence would have been a difficult matter. Indeed, long before the end of our period, conservative tradition was already maintaining features of military architecture as formalities and ornaments divorced from reality. A remarkable and early instance of the traditional rather than the functional castle can be seen at Herstmonceux in Sussex (33), built in the 1440s and restored in the present century. Here again the gatehouse is the most serious military feature, but otherwise the thin walls and slender towers of this beautiful brick-built structure give the lie to an imposing external appearance superficially reminiscent of the neighbouring Bodiam. Some hundred and fifty years later the proud name of castle was taken even more in vain by Longford Castle in Wiltshire; a great house of the 1590s built on a triangular plan and embellished with three cylindrical towers—one at each corner—which were no more than consciously archaic eccentricities. The architects of Herstmonceux and Longford can have had scarcely more expectation that their work would be the object of a full-scale attack than had Anthony Salvin, who, in the middle of the nineteenth century, was commissioned by the first Lord Tollemache

to build the remarkable reproduction of a medieval castle at Peckforton in Cheshire.

In thus following out the development of new buildings through the phase of the fortified manor to the Tudor country mansions with their faint echoes of a past military tradition, we have left behind the great castles standing in their hundreds throughout the English kingdom of the early fourteenth century. It is an even stronger proof of the declining military importance of the castle that they, no less than the new buildings of the period, show in their development—or perhaps we should say in their decline—during the roughly defined period 1350–1550, an ever-increasing concentration upon domestic amenities at the expense of fortification.

Of course in so broad a generalisation, covering so wide an area of space and time, we shall find exceptions, though exceptions, generally speaking, they remain. Lancaster received its present gatehouse in *c*. 1405, and Warwick provides an excellent example of the strengthening of an existing castle in the late fourteenth century and of the fortification of that period at its best. At Warwick the work consisted of the rebuilding of the north side of the bailey of the castle towards the town, with a gatehouse in the centre and a flanking tower at each end. The gatehouse is a fine specimen of the now perfected and traditional plan of a pair of flanking towers, one on either side of the actual gate, bound together into a solid building above the entrance passage. In this instance there are three storeys above the entrance level, and lofty, embattled turrets rise at each corner above the embattled parapet of the roof. In front of the gatehouse itself a barbican is built out, consisting simply of parallel embattled walls with a lesser tower at the end of each, facing the field. Though the long, narrow and hazardous entrance passage thus formed was defended by its gates and portcullis, two drawbridges, and the *meur-*

trières or apertures in the vaults above it at either end, the most striking feature of the whole structure is that the entrance and approach are covered by scientifically disposed triple battlements—those of the barbican, those of the parapet of the gatehouse and those of the latter's turrets which, commanding the whole, were joined together by flying bridges for intercommunication. The two towers, Caesar's Tower and Guy's Tower, which stand at either end of the new work at Warwick, are considered masterpieces of fourteenth-century military architecture, and are still two of the most striking features of this great castle. Both are strong, lofty and machicolated in accordance with the best techniques of contemporary military architecture. Guy's Tower is multi-angular; Caesar's Tower, perhaps the finer of the two, is of peculiar shape, tri-lobed rather like a clover leaf. It stands upon a massive plinth, and rises to a height of one hundred and thirty-three feet, capped by the double system of battlements afforded by its roof-level parapet and the machicolated, embattled parapet encircling the tower some distance below.

It is significant, however, that while this military work was carried out on the north side of the bailey at Warwick, on the south-east side, above the river, the great hall and other domestic apartments of the castle were also rebuilt in the late fourteenth century on more spacious and more comfortable lines. In the same period, at neighbouring Kenilworth and at royal Windsor (37), works were in hand which virtually converted those proud fortresses to palaces no less proud, and which, though exceptionally lavish in their scale, are yet symbolic of the general domestication of the castle in the last two centuries of its history. The work of Edward III at Windsor we shall have occasion later to discuss in detail (pp. 132–5). At Kenilworth under Edward's son, John of Gaunt, Duke of Lancaster, the north and west sides of the inner bailey were rebuilt with a splendid series of residential buildings. Chief among them was the magnificent great hall, which, even in its present ruins, seems not only to contrast with the grim Norman keep of the Clintons hard by, but to overwhelm it with good living, to form a setting fit indeed to the state of the great prince who built it, and to reflect still the sumptuous elegance of the sophisticated age of Froissart and the enigmatic, aesthetic and for all time unfortunate Richard II.

It is especially interesting to notice that amongst the military and quasi-military architecture of the fourteenth and fifteenth centuries we still find at times the tower keep, or something very like it. One of the most striking examples of such a building added in this period to an existing castle occurs at Warkworth. There, possibly between 1380 and 1390, the first Percy Earl of Northumberland caused to be raised upon the original mound of the ancient stronghold the remarkable keep or tower-house which still stands, in shape like a Greek cross crowned with a lofty central turret. Some fifty years later the surviving and enormously impressive brick-built tower at Tattershall in Lincolnshire (30) was added by Ralph Lord Cromwell (the builder also of Wingfield in Derbyshire) to the thirteenth-century castle which he remodelled. To these examples we may add those of Ashby-de-la-Zouch (c. 1475), and the late fourteenth-century Nunney and Old Wardour, both previously mentioned. The conservatism of these late medieval keeps, or, more properly perhaps, tower-houses, has recently been denied. Certainly they were not anachronisms in their time nor conscious revivals of the tower keeps of old, and Tattershall has affinities with contemporary towers in France and Germany. But from them it is impossible not to see the long line of continuity stretching back, through the fourteenth- and fifteenth-century keeps and pele towers of the far north, the thirteenth- and fourteenth-century keeps of York and Flint, Hopton and Knaresborough, and even some of their contemporary gatehouses, to the great tower keeps which dominate twelfth-century castles, and so finally to the Conqueror's keeps at Colchester and the Tower of London. Indeed, though the twelfth and early thirteenth centuries were the classic age of the tower keep, the idea of one concentrated strongpoint within the castle never thereafter entirely disappeared, and that this should also have been the residence of the lord of the castle was natural enough. Though the elaborate fortification of the whole *enceinte* of the greater Edwardian castles in Wales rendered redundant in them the keep as one ultimate strongpoint, such extensive fortification was vastly expensive and, in the later Middle Ages, no longer considered necessary. A tower, on the other hand, was in any period the most obvious form of defensible residence, the simplest but also the most impressive means of drawing strength and comfort together into a small space. The tower-houses of the fourteenth and fifteenth centuries, however, show generally the same growing supremacy of comfort over strength characteristic of other military architecture of the period, and in this emphatically differ from the older tower keep. At Warkworth the walls at their upper levels are pierced by large window openings, and the tower contains an elaborate and ingenious arrangemens of comfortable apartments. Similarly, the original strength of Tattershall, in spite of its fine machicolated parapet and general impressive appearance, can never have been great. Sumptuously appointed within, its entrances, in spite of a forebuilding now gone, were never well defended, and again its window openings are too many and too large for the slings and arrows of any outrageous fortune.

Elsewhere the elaboration of purely residential buildings, hitherto cramped and confined by the overwhelming necessities of defence, is increasingly the measure of new work at existing castles, after the manner, though not always on the scale, of Kenilworth and Windsor. Thus at the episcopal castle of Durham the later fourteenth century saw the enlargement of the hall by Bishop Hatfield (1345–1381), and, of his successors in the see, Bishop Fox (1494–1501) built the enormous kitchen, still in use, and Bishop Tunstall (1530–59) added the present chapel. Similarly at Berkeley, at Ludlow, at Tutbury and at castles throughout the realm, continuous expansion of residential buildings took place with very little addition to, and sometimes little enough maintenance of, existing defences. At Warkworth, in the later fifteenth century, even the great tower-house just described was found insufficiently convenient for its lords (or perhaps their ladies), and, though but recently completed, was largely abandoned in favour of a more roomy mansion in the bailey—formed by the drastic conversion and expansion of the existing thirteenth-century residential buildings there. At Windsor, once again, the soaring and magnificent structure of St. George's chapel (37), begun towards the close of the fifteenth century, could never have been contemplated in a building still regarded as a military strongpoint, and no contrast could be greater than that which it affords with the grim little twelfth-century chapel in the bailey at Ludlow (45).

The steady development of the residential buildings in the medieval castle to the point where, in the fifteenth or sixteenth centuries, they break free from military restrictions, is seldom shown better than at Carew in Pembrokeshire. Within the present ruin of this composite quadrangular castle, typical in showing stonework of almost every period, the comparatively cramped thirteenth-century residential buildings on the east side stand in pointed contrast to the spacious, well-lighted great hall on the west, built in the fifteenth century by Sir Rhys ap Thomas. But while even this hall is still sheltered by the earlier curtain wall, the sixteenth-century residential additions, made by Sir John Perrott in the age of the first Elizabeth, break right through the original *enceinte* of the castle. The juxtaposition of these buildings, with their long line of graceful and entirely civilian mullioned windows, and the powerful, spurred, thirteenth-century drum tower to which they join on the west, is eloquent of the vanished military importance of the castle and its resultant transformation into a palatial and peaceful country mansion (35). The same point is made, to name one example of the many possible, by the fine range of Renaissance buildings raised in the bailey at Dudley by the Earl of Northumberland in the reign of Mary Tudor. Perhaps, however, for the *reductio ad absurdum* of the expansion of the residential buildings within the castle, we must turn to Berry Pomeroy in Devon. For there, incongruously placed within, and indifferent to the fortifications of the medieval castle which surround it, there rose a complete Tudor mansion, begun by the Protector Somerset in the reign of the boy king Edward VI. It is a strange irony of history that this of all buildings should have been in the end shattered by the chances of war which it seemingly ignored, yet it was severely damaged in the Civil War of the seventeenth century, was soon after abandoned, and stands now an empty shell.

The declining military importance of the castle during the period which we have roughly defined as 1350 to 1550 was reflected architecturally by its increasing domestication, until in the end that combination of military and residential rôles which was the essential feature of the medieval castle was broken, and the residence and the military fort became distinct and separate. Fortification, of course, did not cease, but the defences put up by Henry VIII along the south coast in the 1540s against possible French invasion, Deal, Walmer, Camber, St. Mawes or Pendennis, are purely military fortresses. They reflect, too, the more or less established supremacy of gunpowder by this time in being principally solid gun emplacements, and they reflect the changed political structure of the kingdom in being exclusively royal, or in other and more modern terms, forts raised by the government for national defence. By contrast, some of the ancient castles of the realm, considered militarily obsolete, were falling into decay, more especially, perhaps, those outlying royal castles which were losing also their residential importance as our kings abandoned the ceaseless peregrinations of the kingdom undertaken by their medieval predecessors and settled more permanently in London. A survey of Carlisle drawn up in 1529 shows the keep and gatehouse in disrepair through the decay of their roofs, even the chapel and kitchens falling into ruin, and the great hall 'like to fall'. In many of our castles the decay and neglect, then beginning, long continued, to reduce them to the ruins, romantically pleasing but historically depressing, which they now are, and it is sadly instructive to compare the Elizabethan-planned elevation of Tickhill with the present state of that castle. Elsewhere fate has been kinder and, of the many English castles still standing complete and inhabitable, such great medieval fortresses as Warwick or Windsor (37), Arundel or Durham, seen especially from the air, are striking embodiments of the continuity of English life, their stonework of every period still following the original Norman motte-and-bailey earthwork foundations though they have long been transformed into peaceful but stately residences.

6

Castle-building

In the last four chapters we have traced the architectural development of the English castle from its Norman origins in the mid-eleventh century to the triumphant culmination of the late thirteenth and early fourteenth centuries, and thereafter the slow decline. The description of medieval castles or, better by far, the contemplation of any of them for ourselves, inevitably raises the question of how these things were done and by what sort of men. In recent years historians have paid a good deal of attention to the practical side of medieval architecture, that is to say, to the actual process of building as opposed to mere architectural description. The method used has been the very desirable one of combining with the examination of the buildings themselves the study of the written records relating to their construction. In consequence, though much work remains to be done, we are beginning to know something of the cost of medieval building in terms of money, time, labour and materials, to see something of the complex organisation which lay behind it all, and to appreciate more fully both the finished results as we see them and the high degree of skill, scientific and artistic, which produced them. The study of the documentary evidence of architecture has also the immediate value of enabling surviving buildings to be dated with far more accurary than can ever be achieved by the rather hazardous evidence of their physical appearance, while it provides also fascinating information about those many medieval buildings now lost or altered out of all recognition. Finally, not the least exciting result of such studies has been to dispel a little of the cherished anonymity of the Middle Ages, to establish in some measure who built what, and to add to the roll of English architects, which too commonly began with Inigo Jones or Wren, some of the names of the consummate masters of the medieval past.

Here our concern is only with castle-building. Yet of all forms of building none is perhaps more characteristic of the Middle Ages, and certainly none is more exclusively confined to them, ending for all practical purposes with them. And though in most architectural histories medieval churches and cathedrals have received more publicity than the castles, which cannot compete in aethestic beauty, certainly the latter lack nothing in interest, while the worldly magnificence of a Caerphilly, a Conway, a Beaumaris or a Bodiam, called for no less planning, effort and skill than the ecclesiastical splendours of Canterbury, York, Durham or Ely. In a book of this kind no comprehensive account of castle-building could be attempted even if the information were readily available, but some comment upon what is known or conjectured, and some few examples of works done for which written evidence survives, may suffice to take us behind the scenes of medieval military architecture, and do something towards answering the questions of how much the castle cost, how long it took to build, what amount and sort of labour it employed, and who were the craftsmen who planned and directed its construction.

Though the fact must not be allowed to detract from their contemporary strength and efficiency, it is obvious that the early Norman castles of earthwork and timber, of the motte-and-bailey type, compared with their great successors in stone, were relatively simple, quick and cheap to construct. A quite small force of unskilled labour would suffice, directed by some Norman lordling who, having skilfully chosen the site, could adequately control the work. The Bayeux Tapestry vigorously portrays a scene that must have been enacted all over England with the coming of the Normans, in its representation of the raising of the castle at Hastings in 1066 (5). A number of labourers are busily at work digging and throwing up the mound, under the direction of a Norman noble, who may well be count Robert of Mortain, the Conqueror's half-brother. Two of the labourers are apparently settling a difference with their spades behind count Robert's back. The time required to make the motte-and-bailey castle at least militarily efficient was short, though no doubt at a later stage more skilled and more leisurely carpentry would be required to build anything like the elaborate timber house described as standing upon the motte at Ardres in France (p. 30). Ordericus Vitalis implies that the castle at York was thrown up in eigth days during King William's visit to the city in 1069, and whether or not this is literally true, nothing emerges more strikingly from the reading of contemporary chronicles than the speed and ease with which castles were raised by kings and barons alike in the first century of the Norman Conquest. Nor can the cost of this type of castle-building have been considerable. Indeed in the earliest days we may be fairly certain that forced labour supplied the necessary man-power, and the unfortunate English were compelled to raise the symbols and guarantees of their continued conquest. We have heard before the cry of the Peterborough chronicler, writing in the civil war of Stephen's reign in the early twelfth century: '... they filled the land full of castles. They grievously oppressed the wretched men of the land with castle-works.' The same lament seems heard in the Anglo-Saxon Chronicle's summary of the reign of William the Conqueror: 'Castles he caused to be made, and poor men to be greatly oppressed.' In course of time the raising of forced labour became constitutionally respectable, by being attached to the ancient obligation upon Saxon tenantry to aid works upon fortifications and bridges, and later still was replaced by monetary taxation. In the eleventh and twelfth centuries beneficiaries of charters thought in worth-while to include exemption from 'castle-works' amongst the privileges they bargained for and bought from the king, and in the later twelfth century we find unmistakable references in official records to the raising of special local taxation to help finance government fortification—a process which may seem curiously familiar to modern readers.

By contrast to the raising of relatively simple motte-and-bailey fortresses, castle-building in stone was an undertaking vastly more serious and complex, demanding not only skilful siting and planning, but also more specialised and skilful workmanship and craftsmanship, as the castle became increasingly elaborate. There is again a modern ring in a contemporary chronicler's description of building at the Tower of London in the earlier years of Henry II's reign. The work, he writes, was carried out 'with so many smiths, carpenters and other workmen, working so vehemently with bustle and noise that a man could hardly hear the one next to him speak'. Elaborate building in stone was also necessarily slower and was vastly expensive. The reduction in the overall number of English castles, which historians have noted during the twelfth century, though it owed something to the established security of the Norman Conquest, and something to the determined and successful attempts of Henry II to reduce the number of potentially dangerous baronial fortresses, was probably caused above all by the brute economic fact of the greatly increased cost of fortification. Stone castles could not be raised with the gay abandon of the first, fine, careless rapture of Norman hegemony, nor could all the castles then founded be brought up to date by the addition of stone defences and buildings, and many thus grew obsolete and were abandoned.

Though the absence of written evidence must not blind

us to the quite considerable amount of stone fortification carried out in the first century after the Norman Conquest —a period to which, after all, the great square keeps of the Tower of London, Colchester, Rochester, Carlisle and Castle Hedingham, Corfe and Norwich all belong—it is very fortunate that the late twelfth and early thirteenth centuries, the first great period of stone fortification, in which the transition from the castle of earth and timber to the castle of stone was most concentrated, was also a period in which the king's government, followed in time by the officials of the great magnates, increasingly adopted the habit of keeping written records of their transactions. The English medieval state, it may be noted, was amongst the first to adopt the systematic creation and keeping of written records and to establish an efficient bureaucracy. The records which survive from this early period are for the most part royal, but from them we can see at least the king's castleworks in progress, and we can take these works as standards of reference for private and baronial building. The earliest and most important royal records for our purpose are the so-called Pipe Rolls, the Great Rolls of the Exchequer which, beginning even earlier, survive in majestic and almost unbroken series from the second year of King Henry II in 1155–6 to their final abolition in 1832. These rolls, made up for each year by the Exchequer, the financial department of the king's government, contain the record of at least part of the royal revenues and at least part of the royal expenditure therefrom. Year after year upon the Pipe Rolls of Henry II and his sons Richard I and John work upon royal castles throughout the realm is entered, and castle-building expenditure soon becomes and remains by far the heaviest single continuous item of recorded royal expenditure, frequently reaching totals of over £1,000 a year and sometimes soaring to £2,000, £3,000 and even £4,000.

At first sight these figures may seem more amusing than impressive, but they represent very large sums in the valuable money of the time. The average annual income of King Henry II, which means in practice the revenue of the then English government, has been reckoned as perhaps some £20,000. An American historian, Professor Sidney Painter, recently calculated the regular annual income of one of the richest subjects of the Crown in the early thirteenth century, Roger de Lacy, Constable of Chester, whose family were soon to become earls of Lincoln, to be some £800. The same historian found only seven members of the English baronage, who formed the small and immensely powerful ruling class, to have been regularly in receipt, about the year 1200, of over £400 per annum. It was an age in which a knight or lesser country gentleman might live comfortably on £10 to £20 a year; when Abbot Samson of Bury St. Edmunds was heard to remark, perhaps with the over-confidence of age, that five or six marks a year (a mark was 13s. 4d.) would have adequately supported him as a scholar at the University; when the constable of one of the king's castles might receive no more than £10 or £12 a year to support his dignity and responsibility, and when the chaplain of the same castle might well receive no more than a penny a day for his office.

Of the many castleworks of that great builder King Henry II, for which the Pipe Rolls provide us with information, we may perhaps turn first to Orford. For at Orford on the Suffolk coast King Henry built an entirely new castle, that is to say one raised from its foundations in one operation upon a site previously unfortified, and therefore the work is more convenient to use as an example of castlebuilding than the more normal process of adding piecemeal stone buildings and fortifications to an existing site. Moreover, the keep at least of Orford still stands (11) to give point to the record of its building, and, though this keep itself is unique in its design (p. 52), the whole castle as Henry left it must have been typical enough of the keep-and-bailey castles then in vogue. The building of Orford began probably in 1165, for on the Pipe Roll of 1165–6 there occur for the first time entries 'in the work of the castle of Orford', and the total recorded expenditure for the year was over £660—a very large sum, and the largest recorded annual outlay upon a single castle, indeed, since the beginning of the reign. The next year £323 was spent, and by this time, the autumn of 1167, the building, after an outlay of nearly £1,000 in two years, must have been well advanced, for the same roll records payments of some £2 for stocking the castle and 20 marks to Bartholomew de Glanville as custodian of it. Work, however, continued over the next six years, until 1173 when its completion is indicated by the recorded expenditure of £58 2s. 8d., 'in the work of one great ditch round the castle of Orford with palisades and brattices and in the work of a stone bridge in the said castle'. The total recorded expenditure upon the building of Orford between 1165 and 1173 amounts to just over £1,400, and the work was apparently completed in eight years—in significant contrast to the eight days alleged to have sufficed for the raising of the Conqueror's castle at York a hundred years before. It is probably more accurate to express the time taken to build Orford as eigth seasons rather than eight years, for medieval building especially was seasonal of necessity, the work being concentrated in the spring, summer and autumn, and slacking off greatly during the winter months.

Orford was a great castle, important to the king, and incorporating a tower keep of very advanced design, yet it is interesting to see that it incorporated also in its outer defences timber stockades. Their presence emphasis the overwhelming military importance of the keep in the late twelfth-century castle—symbolically emphasised in this case by the fact that of Orford Castle the keep now alone remains. The information about the building on the Pipe Rolls is very summarised and provides few details of how the work was carried out, but the mention on the roll of 1167-8 of finished timbers, presumably for the joists and flooring of the keep, brought from as far away as Scarborough in Yorkshire, where another royal keep was then building, together with the archaeological evidence that some of the stone in the keep at Orford comes from Caen in Normandy, are indications of the complex organisation behind such large-scale building works. Of the architect, craftsmen and labour responsible for the design and execution of the castle, the Pipe Rolls unfortunately tell us nothing, and though it has sometimes been suggested that a certain Master Alnoth, a well-known engineer and architect of Henry II, was responsible, there is in fact no evidence to show that he was in any way connected with it.

Though the cost of any building work must vary in accordance with its scale, the nature of the site, the availability of labour and materials and so on, and though it would be hazardous to assume that the recorded figure of £1,413 10s. 10d. represents the complete total of actual expenditure upon Orford, that figure is a useful indication of the cost of a powerful keep-and-bailey castle newly built in the late twelfth century. Certainly it compares well enough with the known recorded costs of other royal castleworks of about the same date. The main strength of Orford lay in its keep, and the keep at Newcastle upon Tyne, building between 1167 and 1178, seems to have cost some £1,000, while Henry II's completion of the smaller keep at Bowes in Yorkshire (c. 1170–1187) cost just under £600. Again, the recorded cost of the whole new castle at Odiham, built by King John a little later in a period of rapidly rising prices, amounts to about £1,000. But of all the royal castleworks of the late twelfth and early thirteenth centuries in England, one, and that the greatest, far outstrips all others in the amount of treasure and labour lavished upon it. A castle had existed at Dover from at least the earliest days of the Norman Conquest, but the new work carried out chiefly under Henry II and completed in the first years of the reign of Richard Cœur de Lion, his son, was in fact the entire rebuilding of the castle, and comprised the great square tower keep and the towered walls of the present inner bailey, both of which still stand largely unaltered, and a section of the outer curtain to the northeast (36). The work appears to have occupied the years 1179 to 1191, and upon it the Pipe Rolls record an expenditure hitherto unparalleled. Totals of over £1,000 are recorded for this castle alone in each of the three years 1183 –6, and the total figure for the whole period of rebuilding amounts to over £6,800, or in round figures some £7,000.

Amongst the summary entries upon the rolls relating to the building of Dover we are told once or twice of 'the work of the wall round the castle', *i.e.* the outer curtain, and of the wall 'about the tower', *i.e.* the inner curtain about the inner bailey, but over and over again of 'the work of the tower of Dover', *i.e.* the great rectangular tower keep itself which absorbed so large a proportion of the total expenditure and which still dominates the castle (p. 49). Though again the Pipe Rolls afford little detail of the precise way in which the work was carried out, we hear of timber and lead brought in from East Anglia, and, most interesting of all, of the payment year by year of a certain Maurice the Engineer, who appears to have been in charge of the work. This Maurice the Engineer can probably be identified with the Maurice the Mason who is associated on the Pipe Rolls with the building of the keep at Newcastle upon Tyne a few years before, and he is presumably the royal architect responsible both for that fine tower and for the new castle, including the keep, at Dover. If so,

the long-forgotten Maurice leaps at once to the fore-front
of English military architects, and at Dover, especially,
could have no grander monument. Dover in the late twelfth
century, both by the evidence of the treasure poured out
upon it and the still surviving strength of the works of
Henry II and his architect, must have been amongst the
very finest castles in the realm, and well worthy of Matthew
Paris's famous epithet, 'the key of England'.

One other royal castle of the late twelfth century, however, at least rivalled Dover both in its cost and in its finished strength. Though standing in France, at Andeli upon
the Seine on the borders of Normandy, Richard I's beloved Château-Gaillard (p. 64; 19), as the finest contemporary castle in Western Christendom, and one raised by
a King of England in what were then his dominions,
would demand our attention even if the amount of surviving evidence concerning its construction, together with the
majesty of its present remains, did not make it an outstanding example of a major work of military architecture carried out with all the resources of an early medieval state.
'All previous efforts', writes Professor Sir Maurice Powicke
of Richard's fortification in Normandy, 'were cast into the
shade . . . when Château-Gaillard rose on the rock of Andeli
with the unhurried speed and confidence of some magical
creation.' Even more impressive than the cost of the operation was the speed with which it was carried through. A
necessary preliminary, from Richard's point of view, was
the acquisition of the site by the dispossession of the Archbishop of Rouen in whose territory it lay. The result of this
move was an ecclesiastical interdict upon the Duchy of
Normandy, the prohibition of most church services, and
the chronicler Roger of Hoveden tells of 'the unburied
bodies of the dead lying in the streets and squares of the
cities of Normandy'. Even before the fulminating archbishop had been pacified by rich gifts of lands elsewhere,

and the interdict lifted, Richard had begun his building, and thereafter it was pressed on with ruthless but efficient speed. The chronicler William of Newburgh tells the story of how, when in May 1198 the king, as was his custom, was inspecting and urging on the work, a shower of blood fell from the sky. The king's companions were much alarmed by what they took to be an evil portent. But, says the chronicler, 'the king was not moved by this to slacken one whit the pace of the work, in which he took such keen pleasure that, unless I am mistaken, even if an angel had descended from heaven to urge its abandonment he would have been roundly cursed'. In the event, the whole operation, castle and fortified town, seems largely to have been accomplished within the short period 1197–8 at a recorded cost of some £11,500—a truly remarkable achievement whose spurring cause was the urgent military necessity of the defence of Normandy against the growing power of Philip Augustus, King of France.

One of the most interesting features of the story of Château-Gaillard from our point of view is that the building accounts, which survive upon the Norman Exchequer Roll for 1197–8, in contrast to contemporary accounts upon the English Pipe Rolls, are sufficiently detailed to show us for the first time something of the organisation and labour involved in such a work. They tell us of the quarry-men and roughmasons who worked the stone from the quarries, and the freemasons who fashioned it for the walls and towers; of the wood-men who cut the timber, the carters who brought it to the site, and the carpenters who then used it for joists and floors and roofs. They tell us of the miners who cut the ditches and hacked out cellars in the solid rock; of smiths at their forges, lime workers, hodmen, watchmen and soldiers to guard the works; and of clerks who checked materials and expenditure and prepared the accounts. No architect is mentioned by name and it may be there was none in the professional sense, for all authorities are agreed on Richard's personal interest in and direction of the work, into which he poured the experience of a life-time's soldiering and the lessons of fortification learnt in the East. 'Behold, how fair is this year-old daughter of mine!' he is said to have exclaimed when the castle was completed, and we are told he was so pleased with its design as to boast that he could hold it if its walls were made of butter. His charters and correspondence sent out from the new castle, which became his favourite residence in the last two years of his life, are proudly dated 'Apud Bellum Castrum de Rupe' (At the Fair Castle of the Rock), and a fair castle indeed it was. It is a sad outcome of so much expenditure of treasure, effort and genius, that within six years of these events Normandy fell, and with it, cut off and after a heroic defence, the proud castle of Château-Gaillard, though the royal architect, happily perhaps, did not live to see that day.

Great as was the cost and great the finished strength of Dover and Château-Gaillard in the late twelfth century, both are surpassed in either respect by the massive strength and towering prices of Edward I's castles in Wales a century later. The total cost of Harlech (23) was some £9,500; of Conway (21), some £14,000 between 1283 and 1287 when the main work was accomplished; of Beaumaris (24) some £14,400; and of Carnarvon (22) no less than £27,000. In all, it has been estimated that Edward I spent upon the building of his eight Welsh castles some £80,000 in twenty-five years, and even this figure does not represent the final bill, for at Beaumaris and Carnarvon work continued into the reign of his grandson Edward III. In part the high level of this expenditure, which far outstrips anything hitherto recorded, is due to the rising prices of the thirteenth century, and in part is explained by the fact that five of Edward's castles, Conway and Carnarvon amongst them, were combined with new fortified towns. But also it directly reflects the great advances made in military architecture in that same century, and the change in the whole design and concept of the castle. So great an outlay of treasure has been described by Professor J. G. Edwards as 'the premium that Edward paid to insure his Welsh conquests against the fire of rebellion', for the raising of these castles resulted from the conquest of Wales and was designed to perpetuate it. The urgency of military necessity also, as at Château-Gaillard, lies behind the speed with which the work was in the main carried through. Here Beaumaris (1295–c. 1330) and Carnarvon (1283–c. 1330) are exceptional, the building of the former being spread over thirty-five years, and that of the latter being accomplished in three instalments spread unequally over nearly fifty years. Amongst the others, Flint (p. 63) was raised in the eight and a half years from 1277 to 1286, Harlech in the seven and a half years 1283–1290, Builth in the five and a half years 1277–1282, and Rhuddlan (p. 82) in four and a half years between the same dates. Most striking in the concentration of labour involved was Conway, raised in the five years between 1283 and 1287. None of these time-figures, considered separately, it is true, can rival the achievement of Richard I at Château-Gaillard, but the measure of King Edward I's achievement is that his tremendous effort was not concentrated upon one castle but upon eight. Aberystwyth, Builth, Flint and Rhuddlan were going up together from 1277, Harlech, Conway and Carnarvon together from 1283, and long before the last of these was finished work upon Beaumaris had begun. The eight royal Edwardian castles in Wales, which include among their number some of the finest castles ever raised in this country, taken together form one defensive system and one comprehensive undertaking which is by far the greatest single achievement in the history of English castle-building.

We are fortunate in the possession, not only of the Pipe Rolls but also of a large number of other and more detailed accounts and other documents relating to the building of Edward I's castles in Wales. These records, like most surviving medieval records, are not complete, but taken together they shed a flood of light upon the way in which this great operation was carried through. They show clearly the seasonal character of medieval building, and they show also another general fact which presumably holds good for stone-building in other centuries of the Middle Ages, namely that wages account for some two-thirds of the total cost of the work. But perhaps the most exciting revelation made by these accounts, over and above the great cost of the work which they show, is the size and composition of the labour force involved. At Harlech in the summer of 1286 an average weekly number of nearly one thousand men were employed. The three castles of Conway, Carnarvon and Harlech employed between them an average of some two thousand five hundred in each week of the seasons 1285–7. At Beaumaris alone in the summer of 1295 about three thousand five hundred men were at work. Perhaps no other figures show more clearly the scale of these great works and the capacity of medieval enterprise and administrative ability. And impressive as these figures are by any standard, it is to be remembered that they must be set against an English population of perhaps three to four millions. To mobilise so great a force of labourers and craftsmen it is scarcely too much to say that the countryside was scoured. Not only from Wales and the Marches they came, but from Northumberland and Yorkshire in the north, Nottinghamshire and Northamptonshire in the midlands, Norfolk, Suffolk and Essex in the east, Oxfordshire, Wiltshire, Dorset and Somerset in the south and west, and from other English shires besides. Force was resorted to at times, for medieval kings enjoyed the power of impressment of labour, which was a great advantage to them in their works, though, as on this occasion it must have done, it seriously hindered the private building-works of their subjects. An account of 1277, relating to the bringing of workmen from Yorkshire to Flint and Rhuddlan, records the payment of $7\frac{1}{2}d$. a day for seven days to each of three mounted sergeants, for 'guarding the said workmen for the said seven days lest they flee on the way'.

Amongst the great companies of men assembled by one means and another to work King Edward's will in Wales, we see again the same general categories of craftsmen and workmen made familiar by the accounts for Château-Gaillard a century before—freemasons, roughmasons and quarriers, carpenters and smiths, carters, plumbers, boat-men and a host of miscellaneous labourers. Some worked on piece-work and others on time; a few, the most skilful, had salaries; and all were paid by the ubiquitous, calculating and scribbling clerks. And lastly, among the throng we can distinguish the architects, the master craftsmen in charge of and directing the works. Though Master Walter of Hereford, who had also been master mason at Edward's Cistercian foundation at Vale Royal, was in charge of the later work at Carnarvon from 1295, the man primarily responsible for all these prodigious works was Master James of St. George from Savoy, mason and 'engineer'. Brought to England by Edward, he became 'master of the king's works in Wales', and the castles which he raised there are as much a monument to him as to the monarch he served so well. Afterwards he, with Walter of Hereford, followed the king on his abortive compaigns in Scotland, and he died in or before 1309, to be judged by the sheer measure of his achievement the greatest architect in the history of English medieval castles.

The examples of castle-building so far chosen have been necessarily few and arbitrary, but they have included some of the greatest works undertaken, and with Edward I's operations in Wales we have seen something of the means whereby the finest English castles were raised, and of the wealth, labour and organisation which lie behind the culmination of English medieval military architecture in the late thirteenth century. Though thereafter the military importance of the castle declined, building-works at existing castles or the raising of new fortified places continued. We ought finally to look at one or two of these building-works of the later Middle Ages which, though increasingly concentrated upon domestic amenities, are not thereby necessarily smaller in scale or lacking in interest. Moreover, the examples of building so far used have all been of royal works, whereas in all periods of the Middle Ages the baronage was no less active in castle-building than the Crown. Indeed, the realisation that in the medieval English state private castles commonly outnumbered royal, and not infrequently rivalled them in individual strength, rather argues that the common suggestion of architectural historians, that the Crown and the Church held a near-monopoly in medieval building, is a misleading exaggeration. However this may be, from the later Middle Ages at least, a number of private building accounts have survived to be added to the formidable mass of parchment and paper relating to royal building and the medieval 'Office of Works', and from them we may choose two series concerned with the building of Caister and Kirby Muxloe, both typical fortified manors of the fifteenth century.

Sir John Fastolf, a captain of Henry V's campaigns against France, whose actual character bore no relation at all to the version later dramatised by Shakespeare to the anger and distress of the warrior's descendants, 'exercised', according to William Worcester his herald, 'in the werres contynuelly about xliiij yeres'. Out of his martial profits and experience Caister Castle in Norfolk was built. The

127

castle later passed to the Pastons, and its ruins still stand, marked by their very fine, slender and cylindrical tower. The accounts which have survived, now in the British Museum and recently printed, cover the three years 1432–5 and give a total expenditure of £1,480 5s. 9¼d. They are not, however, complete, and indeed, according to the no doubt exaggerated statement of William Worcester, the building occupied thirty years and cost £6,000. As was so often the case with later medieval fortified manors, a house already stood upon the site, and was now altered, rebuilt and extended beyond all recognition. Of the new buildings and works undertaken the accounts mention the west and north walls, the hall, the chapel and the placing of 'lez deskes' therein, a horse-mill for the bakehouse, and the garden. There were set-backs and mistakes made in the progress of the work, incidents common to building in all ages, and the accountant, William Granour, who was in charge of the administrative side, sought allowance for his expenses on a certain 'counterwall', which had fallen into the moat through a defect of the first foundation. A notable feature of the whole building is that it was chiefly of brick, and indeed Caister is amongst the earliest and finest specimens of medieval brickwork. Accordingly, the accounts are full of references to the bricks which were made on the spot, and the categories of craftsmen mentioned include brickmakers and bricklayers as well as the usual masons and carpenters. No architect is named, and indeed the surviving accounts mention few craftsmen by name, apart from a certain Henry Wood, 'masoun', who failed in his claim to be allowed half a day's wages for his journies between Norwich and his work—'the qwiche [claim]', noted the careful accountant, 'I have disalowd til I have oder comaundement of yow'.

The works at Kirby Muxloe (43) in Leicestershire are of even greater interest. The structure itself is typical of the

25 Kidwelly, Carmarthenshire: the castle of the family of de Chaworth; a concentric castle with a difference

26 Goodrich, Herefordshire. Note the twelfth-century keep in the centre, the semi-circular barbican guarding the entrance (top right) and the spurred drum tower in the foreground

27. The Tower of London: the Conqueror's keep standing at the centre of a great concentric castle

28 Bodiam, Sussex: amongst the latest of southern castles, raised *c.* 1385 on the quadrangular plan (cf. p. 99)

29 (above) Chipch
Northumberland:
northern pele tow

30 (left) Tattershall, I
colnshire: the late me
val tower-house

(right) Little Wen-
Suffolk (c. 1270–80)

THIRTEENTH-
CENTURY
FORTIFIED
MANOR-HOUSES

(below) Stokesay,
ropshire: fortified
by Laurence de
Ludlow (c. 1291)

33   Herstmonceux, Sussex (*c.* 1440)

FIFTEENTH-CENTURY FORTIFIED MANOR-HOUSES

34   Oxburgh Hall, Norfolk (*c.* 1480)

35   Carew, Pembrokeshire, showing Sir John Perrott's work

36 Dover, Kent: the great keep and towered inner bailey (centre,
c. 1179–91) are chiefly the work of Henry II. The old gate is in
the left foreground, the Constable's Gate on the right

fortified manors of the later Middle Ages, and, though it is now referred to by common courtesy as a castle, it is worth noticing that it is never so called on the surviving accounts. Again the building was chiefly of brick, and again it was raised on the site of an existing house, part of which was incorporated in the new work. This new work was begun in 1480 by order of William, Lord Hastings, the great Yorkist leader, it is thought in some emulation of, and rivalry with, the Lancastrian Lord Cromwell's castle at Tattershall (30) in Lincolnshire, begun some fifty years before, also built of brick and its accounts also surviving. But Kirby Muxloe differs entirely in plan from Tattershall and follows instead the quadrangular lay-out with angle towers which we have seen to be much favoured in later medieval military architecture. In this instance the rectangular angle towers are supported by lesser towers, one in the centre of each of three sides; a massive gatehouse, the strongest and most seriously intended part of the building, stands in the middle of the north side; and the whole is surrounded by a wide wet moat. The accounts themselves, conveniently contained in one ledgerbook, are more detailed than any we have so far noticed. From them the progress of the work may be followed not merely year by year but week by week, from its inception in October 1480 to its completion in December 1484—or rather one should say to its end at that date, for the work, as we shall see, was never properly completed.

Operations began in the October of 1480, but, as we would expect, during the following winter months activity was comparatively slight and was principally confined to the clearing and preparation of the site itself and the moat. With the advent of spring the tempo quickens. Large quantities of stone are brought from neighbouring quarries for the foundations, timber is cut and made ready, bricks made and stacked by thousands, and more craftsmen and labourers drafted in. Throughout the summer season of 1481 work was in full swing, with masons, bricklayers and carpenters, carters and common labourers all busy on and about the site. The walls were rising under the bricklayers and work was begun on the two angle towers at the north end of the enclosure. Amongst the stream of entries on the accounts of disbursements at this time for wages and materials, one, recording the payment of 1s. 8d. to a certain Powel and four men, who sat up one night at the end of May to watch lest the water in the moat should rise and flood the site, shows clearly that the English summer has changed its character little in the course of centuries. In the autumn preparations were made for the coming slack winter season, many of the workmen were paid off, nine cartloads of stubble were brought in from the adjacent fields to cover the tops of walls and towers against frost, and at the end of October the accounts were cast up to show a total expenditure over the last twelve months of £330 3s. 0d.

The pattern of work and organisation shown by the accounts for the first twelve months of the building of Kirby Muxloe remains much the same for the following years. The great activity of summer is followed by a slack winter period lasting from about October to March, when the labour force is much reduced and the remaining workmen have their wages lowered to correspond with their shorter hours—though as the building nears completion the contrast between summer and winter becomes less marked, and in all seasons the freemasons could continue to fashion stone in their lodge. The workmen, who all appear by name in the accounts, were drawn from a wide area, some coming from Wales and some of the bricklayers, especially, from East Anglia, the centre of late-medieval brick architecture. All or most were resident upon the site, a chaplain being provided throughout for their spiritual welfare. The more skilled members at least of the medieval building industry followed of necessity an itinerant profession, moving from one work to another. Amongst the company at Kirby Muxloe we may notice especially the master craftsmen, John Hornne and John Corbell, master bricklayers, and John Doyle, master carpenter, each of them paid 8*d.* a day in distinction to the 6*d.* of the ordinary craftsmen and the 4*d.* of the common labourers. The principal master mason, the architect in modern terms, was John Couper, who had previously worked at Eton, Winchester and the church at Tattershall, in each case apparently under William Waynflete, Bishop of Winchester and founder of Magdalen College, Oxford, a great organiser and patron of building. As befitted so important a man, John Couper was not permanently on the site, but visited it from time to time.

In the early summer of 1483, in the midst of all the activity of the third full season, and when the work was beginning to approach completion, a tragedy befell Kirby Muxloe, dramatically reflected even in the matter-of-fact accounts. King Edward IV had died in April, and Lord Hastings, his close supporter, was seized and executed by the usurping Richard, formerly Duke of Gloucester. On the building accounts the busy work comes almost to a stop, and though it was later resumed by the widowed Lady Hastings it was not on the old scale again, and the great building was never completed on the original plan. The total recorded cost from the accounts, which end in December 1484, amounts to just under £1,000, expended upon a dwelling which, like Thornbury in Gloucestershire or Hampton Court, was never enjoyed by the lord who first commissioned it.

In the earlier chapters of this book it was emphasised that the architectural history of the typical English castle was one of gradual and continuous development from an early origin. And since in the first century after the Norman Conquest the castles so freely founded were for the most part of earth and timber only, it follows that great building-works in stone devoted to the raising of new castles, such as we have so far described, though they are the most interesting, are not the most typical works of medieval military architecture. Castle-building works in the Middle Ages, viewed as a whole, most commonly took the form of the improvement and extension of existing fortresses. The advent of the stone castle itself meant usually the piecemeal addition of stone walls and buildings to motte-and-bailey strongholds, and thereafter such great works of improvement as were carried out at Windsor, Scarborough or Newcastle under Henry II, at the Tower under Richard I, at Kenilworth or Knaresborough under John, at Winchester or the Tower again under Henry III and Edward I, are more typical of their age than the raising of such new stone castles as Orford or Château-Gaillard. Even Edward I's castles in Wales are exceptional in this sense, arising from the exceptional circumstances of the conquest of Wales and the military necessity of planting new castles in newly acquired territory.

Of all the examples of works for the improvement of existing castles which might be cited, none shows more vividly the scale they might assume than the building commissioned by Edward III at Windsor—his birthplace (on 13th November, 1312) and ever the favoured residence and castle of medieval kings (37). The chronicler Ranulf Higden relates how, 'our lord the King, at the instance of William Wickham, clerk, caused many excellent buildings in the Castle of Windsor to be thrown down, and others more fair and sumptuous to be set up. For almost all the masons and carpenters throughout the whole of England were brought to that building, so that hardly anyone could have any good mason or carpenter, except in secret, on account of the king's prohibition.' The main work falls into two divisions. First, between about 1350 and 1356, the chapel of Henry III, which already stood in the lower bailey, was remodelled and refurbished and extensive buildings were raised near it for the resident canons who were to serve it. The object was to make a fitting ecclesiastical centre for the king's new chivalrous Order of the Garter—though the Knights assemble today in the even finer chapel of St. George, which in turn replaced Edward III's chapel a century later. The second part of the work, which began about 1355 and continued until the king's death in 1377, chiefly comprised the extensive rebuilding of the upper ward and the royal lodgings within it. A new hall was raised, the old hall was converted into a great chamber, a new kitchen and gatehouse were built and new sets of chambers, each including a private chapel, were provided for the king and queen. It is also interesting to notice that even at this late date new buildings, chifly of oak and still in the main surviving, which included hall and private chambers, were built within the shell keep upon the mound —though it would seem they chiefly served as temporary lodgings for the king while more sumptuous and spacious apartments were being constructed in the bailey beneath. We may note, too, that, attention to the keep not-with-standing, the whole work has very little that is military about it, and by it, indeed, Windsor was converted finally from a fortress to the palace it now is.

For all these great operations at Windsor detailed accounts and other documents survive, and have been printed, translated and commented upon at length in the monumental official history of the castle by W. H. St. John Hope. To obtain the necessary labour, the royal power of impressment was brought to bear, and the prerogative of purveyance exercised to bring together the materials. Letters patent dated 26th April, 1350, for example, empower the king's beloved clerk, Richard of Rotheley, surveyor of the works in the castle of Windsor, 'to take and provide masons, carpenters, and other workmen who may be needed for our works aforesaid, wherever they can be found ... the fee of the Church only excepted, and except the workmen already retained for our works at Westminster, our Tower of London and Dartford; also to take and provide stone, timber, and other necessaries for the works aforesaid, and carriage for the same timber and stone and other premises. ...' Amongst the great numbers of labourers and craftsmen at and about the castle in the next near-thirty years, the accounts list freemasons and roughmasons, scapplers and quarriers at the quarries, carpenters and sawyers, plumbers, plasterers and daubers, glaziers and paviers, coopers and tilers, carters and smiths. Amongst this small army, all in receipt of the king's wages willy-nilly, we can distinguish some of the leading architects and craftsmen of the day. The master masons in charge of the work were John Sponle and William of Winford, the last named reckoned also to have been responsible for the west towers of Wells, the existing gatehouse at Abingdon Abbey and perhaps New College, Oxford. Amongst the carpenters were Master William of Hurley, who is known to have been concerned with the stalls in the chapel, and whose other work included the wooden vault to the octagon at Ely Cathedral; William of Wintringham, who was in charge of the building of the great hall roof at Windsor, and Master William Herland, who had worked with Hurley on the lost splendours of St. Stephen's Chapel, Westminster, and whose son Hugh, perhaps the greatest of the English medieval carpenters, was to create the magnificent timber roof which still spans Westminster Hall. Payments upon the accounts of 1352 to 'Master John Lyncoln glazier engaged upon the ordering of the glazing of the windows of the king's chapel', and to 'Master John Athelard glazier working with the same upon the glazing of the said windows', remind us also

134

of another type of medieval craftsman whose craft is now largely lost.

Amongst the constant entries on the accounts for the acquisition and carriage of materials, the great quantities of timber are especially noticeable, used for the roof, stalls and other fittings of the chapel and the roof of the hall, the buildings in the keep and a hundred other purposes. An account of 1354 refers to over three thousand oaks 'accruing from a certain wood at Cagham', and one of 1361–2 to the felling of over two thousand oaks. Amongst the details of the buildings referred to we may mention bath-houses, the queen's 'daunsyng chambre', and mews for the king's falcons, all among the royal apartments; a great clock (most un-military addition) in the keep; and a reredos of carved alabaster for the chapel, brought ready-made in ten carts from Nottingham in 1367, which we would give much to see. In short, this great work at Windsor was carried out on the most lavish scale by a luxury-loving king wielding all the resources of a wealthy, well-organised medieval state—and its cost was prodigious, amounting to some £50,000 between 1350 and 1377, a figure out of all proportion to any other we have seen.

Not all contemporary castles were so luxuriously appointed as Edward III's Windsor (37), nor all so strong in their age as Edward I's castles in Wales, Richard I's Château-Gaillard (19) or Henry II's Dover (36). Yet the sight of Warwick or Alnwick, Caerphilly (20) or Kidwelly (25), emphasises that the lay magnates lagged little if at all behind the Crown in castle-building, and nor, for that matter, did the princes of the Church, as such episcopal castles as Newark or Durham remind us. The medieval castles which still stand in whole or in impressive part throughout the kingdom represents the cumulative labours of close on five hundred years. The type of building work with which we have been concerned in this chapter was reproduced on a greater or lesser scale on countless occasions throughout those centuries, and the building and near-continuous improvement of the hundreds of castles in medieval England and Wales demanded not only creative thought and scientific planning in almost every case, but a highly organised and competent building industry as well. Even in terms of mere maintenance the task was formidable enough. To think of these things broadens the cloistered view, seen through a stained-glass window darkly, of the Middle Ages as simply the 'Age of Faith', which an over-emphasis upon medieval ecclesiastical architecture encourages, while the study of medieval building as a whole drives from the mind any lingering association of the Middle Ages with the Dark Ages. These things were not achieved by simple men inferior in every way to ourselves. Nothing perhaps can put us more directly in touch with our medieval past than its architecture, and certainly no age could desire a more imposing monument to its skill. But now, to come back to the castle itself, which was so uniquely the product to the Middle Ages, we must change our viewpoint and turn to consider what was its rôle in medieval life, and wherein lay its importance, that so much treasure, skill and labour were concentrated upon it.

7

The Castle in War

THE military rôle of the castle is the most obvious, the most romantic, and basically the most important. Though the medieval castle was always a residence no less than a fortress, and though from these two fundamental rôles many secondary uses followed, it was, after all, military necessity which first called the castle into being, whether at its far-off origins in ninth-century France or in the England of the Norman Conquest, and military necessity which caused precisely that fusion of the dwelling and the stronghold which is the peculiar characteristic of the castle. Warfare, in the earlier Middle Ages at least, turned almost exclusively upon the castle, and though from the fourteenth century the castle's military importance began to decline, that decline was gradual and by no means universal. To read of wars in the chronicles of the eleventh, twelfth and thirteenth centuries is to read largely of an interminable series of sieges, while the state records of the kingdom show the preparation of castles for defence to have amongst the major concerns of military organisation—the carrying out of last-minute repairs, the buying up of provisions, the drafting of fighting-men to bring the garrison up to its wartime strength. Moreover, though the rôle of the castle in war was very much more than that of a stronghold in which attack was awaited and subsequently defied, it is sieges which capture the limelight of recorded events, and in resistance to attack that the castle is seen in its most characteristic rôle. Indeed, though the castle served as a base for aggressive military action, though its walls and towers housed the comfortable dwelling of its lord and his household, though it played its part as the administrative centre of wide estates and was used as armoury, treasury or prison, it was considerations of defence first and foremost which governed its design and its architectural development. If therefore we wish to see the castle in action and to begin to understand its importance in contemporary history, or even to understand more fully its architecture, we muct turn first to medieval siege-craft, whose machinations it was the first concern of castle-builders to counter and overcome.

The earliest English castles of earthwork and timber, the motte-and-bailey fortresses which predominated in the first century after the Norman Conquest, were at once an effective answer to the cavalry of mailed knights which then dominated warfare in the west, and a formidable obstacle also to any assault on foot. The account of the capture of the motte-and-bailey castle of Le Puiset in France in the year 1111, which is contained in the 'Life' of Louis the Fat, King of France, written by Abbot Suger, shows well enough such a castle in action against the type of attack then commonly made. The garrison began the operation on the offensive by attempting to drive off their enemy in the field. Only when this failed did they withdraw behind the defences of their palisaded ramparts, from which eminence they showered down missiles upon their assailants. The king's forces concentrated their attentions first upon the castle gate and sought to burn it down. They failed, but the attempt is significant, both in being directed upon the gateway, always a latent weak point inviting attack, and in the employment of fire. In the thirteenth-century romance of Fulk fitz Warin we are told of a fierce assault upon a castle whose gates 'were burnt and destroyed by fire fed with bacon and grease'. Fire was especially the enemy of the timber castle, and we may notice that in the

Bayeux Tapestry illustration of an eleventh-century attack on Dinan, two soldiers are attempting to set fire to the tower on the mound (3). To revert, however, to the immediate affairs of King Louis at Le Puiset, the next phase of the attack took the form of a diversion by a section of the royalist forces under Theobald, count of Chartres, who went round to the other side of the castle and attempted unawares to storm the bailey there. This again failed, partly because of the difficulty of assaulting up the steep sides of the earthen banks, and finally because the garrison delivered a devastating mounted sortie against them, cutting them up and tumbling them into the ditch before riding triumphantly back into the castle. At length the main body of the besiegers, inspired we are told by the example of a priest, made a determined assault across the ditch and up the ramparts, hacked and wrenched their way through the palisade, and carried the bailey. Hugh, the lord of Le Puiset, and those of the garrison who survived, then withdrew to the separate and ultimate stronghold of the castle, the mound. But disheartened no doubt by the loss of the bailey and many of their comrades, they failed either effectively to defend it or to escape to the open country at their back, and soon capitulated to the victorious king.

In affrays of this sort victory was likely to go simply to the better men or the greater number of them, and the motte-and-bailey castle was an adequate stronghold. Yet its strength was clearly greatly inferior to the castle of stone which succeeded it, and in fact the stone castle which became increasingly common in the England of the twelfth century was both the result and the cause of greatly improved methods of attack. These advanced methods and means of attack were not new in the historical sense, but were for the most part the achievements of classical antiquity reintroduced and now increasingly applied. Taken together they involved almost all that the wit of man could

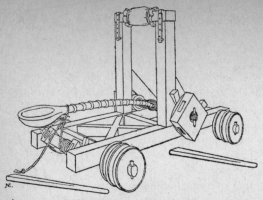

A mangonel, the arm hauled down before loading

devise against prepared positions before the development of explosives, and they made up an art and science of siege-craft which remained largely unchanged from the later twelfth century until almost the end of the Middle Ages; for the introduction of gunpowder into warfare in the fourteenth century had little immediate practical effect. The medieval castle developed in direct response to medieval siege-craft, and rapidly achieved a supremacy of defence over attack within the necessary limits of human endurance and the adequate provision of supplies.

In the Middle Ages as in any other period the methods of attack against a fortified position may be broadly divided under the two heads of bombardment and close assault, though in practice the two are usually complementary to each other. The artillery of the Middle Ages used for bombardment were the great stone-throwing 'engines' of which we hear a great deal both in chronicles and in records. Their chief use was to batter a breach in the defences through which an assault could be made, and, in modern parlance, to 'soften up' the target. Their study is somewhat complicated by the fact that none has survived, and even

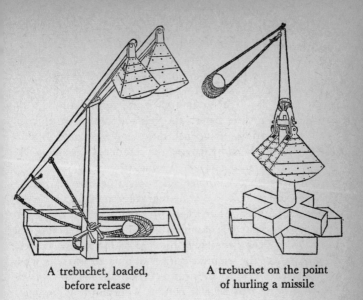

A trebuchet, loaded,
before release

A trebuchet on the point
of hurling a missile

more by the vague and imprecise terminology which contemporaries used to describe them. Briefly, we may limit them to three main types, each with its own method of propulsion, though it is probable that in practice composite machines were devised making use of more than one form of motive power. First, then, was the *mangon* or *mangonel,* which worked on the principle of torsion. A long arm with a cup or sling at its free end passed through a skein of ropes stretched between upright posts. The ropes were twisted towards the target by windlasses, the arm pulled down against their torsion, and a large rock or some other projectile placed in the cup or sling. When released, the free end of the arm was hauled up and over by the torsion of the ropes acting on its lower end, and the projectile was hurled towards the target. A more powerful type of stone-throwing engine was the *trebuchet,* brought into common use, it seems, towards the end of the twelfth century. Here again the rock or other projectile was discharged from the free and longer end of a revolving arm, but in this case the arm was simply pivoted between two upright posts, and the motive power was provided by a great counter-weight at the other and shorter end. In addition to its greater power, the trebuchet was more efficient in action than the mangonel, since its range could to some extent be regulated by moving the counter-weight along the arm or by increasing and decreasing its mass.

Both mangonel and trebuchet might be used, of course, to cast any kind of projectile that came to hand in the exigencies of a hard-pressed siege. In particular they frequently discharged jars or containers of inflammable liquid, the dreaded 'Greek fire' which brought to the medieval scene something of the scientific horrors of modern warfare, while a fourteenth-century illustration of a trebuchet loaded with a dead horse may suggest perhaps a medieval approach to germ warfare. Principally, however, they were stone-throwing engines, or *petrariae* to use a Latin word frequently used to describe either, employed *par excellence* to batter down defences and make a breach. By contrast, the third type of engine, the *ballista* or, to give a later name for the same type of machine, the *springal,* though it might be adapted to cast stones, was most suited to the discharge of iron shafts or javelins. It worked on the principle of tension, the principle, that is, of the bow-and-arrow, and was indeed like an enormous crossbow—though to say this is to put the case in reverse since the hand-crossbow, of which we shall have more to say later, was in fact developed from the *ballista*. Discharging great iron bolts, the *ballista* was generally used not for bombardment but for picking off any of the garrison who showed themselves at battlements or apertures, and with its flatter trajectory it was capable of more accurate aim than either mangonel or trebuchet.

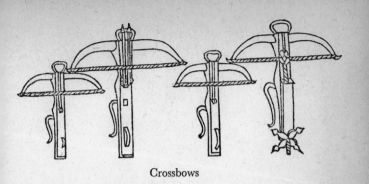

Crossbows

The lineal descendant of these bombarding siege-engines, performing the same function by a different and in the long-run revolutionary method of propulsion, was the cannon. Though not making its appearance until the later Middle Ages, it is most conveniently dealt with at this point. Gunpowder, the 'villainous salt petre' of Hotspur's mincing courtier, appears to have been first introduced into English warfare in the first half of the fourteenth century, and cannon are said to have been used against the Scots in the first year of the reign of King Edward III (1327–77). Our immediate concern is with the use of ordnance in siege-warfare, and here, as indeed with the use of cannon and fire-arms in the field, the essential thing about gunpowder in the Middle Ages is not to exaggerate its importance. A most interesting illumination in a manuscript of about the year 1326 belonging to Christ Church, Oxford (41), is reckoned to be the earliest illustration known of an English cannon. It shows a small thing shaped like a bulbous bottle or flagon, loaded with an iron bolt like a large dart, and lying upon a four-legged stand. A soldier, standing at a respectful distance as well he might, is in the act of firing it with a hot iron bar. Clearly here is no serious threat to the strength and supremacy of the castle. In fact

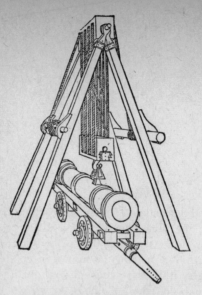

A large bombard or cannon
loaded upon its carriage

early cannon were greatly inferior in every respect to the
tried and powerful siege-engines. They were slow; they
were small; and in the fourteenth century at least they
discharged principally only bolts or garrots, for large pieces
able to discharge stone balls were not yet cast and the iron
cannon-ball lay even further in the future. For long after
the introduction of fire-arms, also, the ballistic force of the
powder used was low—probably deliberately so for fear of
bursting the barrel. In all, early cannon were probably as
dangerous to their users as to the foe, and their chief value
seems to have been their effect upon the morale of the
enemy (and, one imagines, of his horses) rather than any
damage they inflicted upon his person or his defences. In
the fifteenth century, it is true, the development of guns

144

and large ordnance was rapid, and the great Mons Meg still to be seen at Edinburgh Castle dates from about 1460. Such pieces, when available, were highly effective as bombards in siege-warfare. With two great cannon of this sort, named 'Newcastle' and 'London', the Earl of Warwick, the King Maker, after the battle of Hexham in 1464, took Bamburgh Castle, hitherto considered near-impregnable. But it is to be remembered and emphasised that in this country at least ordnance were slow in development and adoption, remained immensely expensive, were by no means readily available when and where they were wanted, and are not to be regarded as an immediate and easy explanation of the decline in the military importance of the castle in the later Middle Ages. It is of the greatest interest in this respect to see that the late-fifteenth-century Italian work upon military science, the *De Re Militari* of Robert Valturius, still gives detailed drawings and descriptions of the trebuchet as well as of cannon and bombards. Only perhaps by the mid-sixteenth century, when our period ends, were cannon both generally effective and extensively employed, and it is instructive to remember that even a century later, in the Civil War of King and Parliament, many English castles (and some largely unfortified houses as well) held out long and heroically against the pounding of Cromwellian guns.

In medieval siege-warfare, in addition to the comparatively long-range artillery of stone-throwing engines or cannon, there were other engines and techniques for breaching walls and towers at close quarters. The crudest and not the least effective instrument for this purpose was the battering-ram, usually the biggest tree-trunk that could be found, capped with iron, swung on ropes, and crashed again and again against masonry or gate until the structure collapsed. Defences sometimes employed by the garrison were the lowering of some form of buffer between the ram and its point of impact, or the skilful dropping of a heavy forked appliance to catch and hold its head. A somewhat more subtle device than the ram, but slower in its effect, was the bore; a smaller instrument with an iron point, employed especially against sharp angles to work away the stones of the masonry piecemeal and thereby make a cavity in wall or tower. The same end could be gained, of course, though with greater labour and exposure, by the simple use of picks and crow-bars, and we are told that at the siege of Acre during the Third Crusade King Richard I offered cash rewards to those of his soldiers who succeeded in wresting a stone from the walls of the doomed city.

But the most efficient method of bringing down a portion of wall or tower to gain an entry was by undermining, and the mine was, with good reason, the most dreaded device of medieval siege-craft. The miners, often enough well-paid professionals, dug and tunnelled their way down beneath the foundations which they under-pinned with stout timber props. The mine chamber was then filled with brushwood or other combustible material, and, when all was ready, fire was applied and the miners withdrew. The props having been burnt, the masonry above collapsed, and the waiting assailants poured through the gap. Only the castle built upon a rock, or one surrounded by the broadest of well-filled moats, was immune from this deadly and most nerve-racking form of attack. Against it there was no remedy save the hazardous process of the counter-mine —an attempt by the besieged to tunnel down into the mine from their side and capture it—which even if successfully directed could only result in a desperate, cramped, hand-to-hand encounter in a dark and choking underground cavity. There are few more dramatic examples of the devastating effect of the mine in this country than King John's use of it at Rochester in 1215. Having taken the bailey of the castle, John found himself held up by the massive

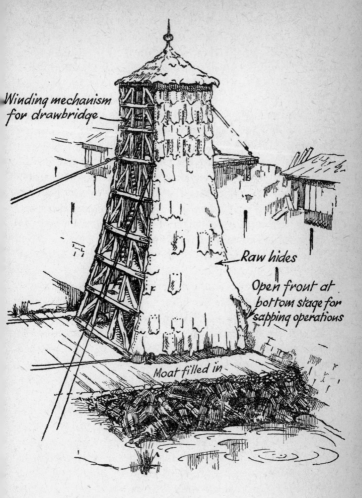

Winding mechanism for drawbridge

Raw hides

Open front at bottom stage for sapping operations

Moat filled in

A belfry

strength of the keep which proved well-nigh impervious to the battering of his siege-engines. Accordingly he called in his miners, who succeeded in bringing down one whole corner of that great tower, still today one of the most impressive keeps in the kingdom. A royal writ enrolled upon the surviving Close Roll, addressed to Hubert de Burgh the king's Justiciar, and dated at Rochester on 25th November, 1215, gives us a vivid glimpse of the details of the mining operation. 'We command you', it runs, 'that with all haste, by day and night, you send to us 40 bacon pigs of the fattest and those less good for eating to bring fire under the tower'—that is, to fire the mine. In fact, the monument to those forty pigs still remains in the one rounded corner and cylindrical angle turret of the keep at Rochester—built up in the next reign, in the latest fashion and in contrast to the rectangular plan of the rest of the tower, to make good the ravages of John's miners (9).

Breaching the defences of the stone castle, by whatever means, was always a long, skilled and laborious process, and to the end of the castle's active history assault by escalade, i.e. by the simple but hazardous use of scaling ladders, remained a much-employed method of forcible entry. A common elaboration of this form of assault, also, was the use of the belfry or great movable tower (p. 147). Pushed up against the castle walls it enabled an attack to be delivered upon their summit with a much greater concentration of force than the one-man-at-a-time technique of the ladder. The belfry, moreover, had other valuable uses, for in addition to being an elevated platform for launching attacks, it could serve as a look-out post, or firing platform, commanding even the interior of the beleaguered castle. Thus, at the siege of Bedford in 1224, the young King Henry III commanded such a great wooden tower to be raised and manned by archers and crossbowmen, and so effective was it that, according to the chronicler Roger of

An ingenious, but probably dangerous,
device for gaining the ramparts

Wendover, no member of the garrison could remove his armour without being mortally wounded.

We have noticed that broad water defences, such as existed at Kenilworth or Caerphilly, were almost the sole artificial protection against the mine, and even the more normal and modest moat or ditch was amongst the most vital defences of the castle, for a portion at least had to be filled in with infinite labour, or adequately bridged, before ram, bore or belfry could be brought up to the walls, or indeed before almost any form of assault could be launched. Even so, the ram and the bore and the men working them needed protection from the assailants above, and this was commonly supplied by large movable penthouses, under cover of which they moved up to the walls and operated upon them. The penthouse, too, was used as cover for the entrance to the mine if this was made close up to the castle.

The penthouses themselves, and also the belfries and the stone-throwing engines, were commonly covered with raw hides, or sometimes metal plates, for being constructed of timber they were otherwise inflammable, and were the chosen target of the garrison's Greek Fire. Fire, indeed, played a large part in medieval sieges and warfare in general, and the age-old phrase 'with fire and sword' is based on an age-old practice. Lastly, we must notice that many of the engines and devices of siege-craft were commonly given fanciful names, sometimes derived from classical antiquity, which, loosely used by chroniclers not always well versed in military matters, give to the whole subject a romantic sounding confusion. Thus the movable penthouse sheltering ram or bore may be called a 'tortoise' or 'cat' from its slow or stealthy approach. The same word 'cat' seems also to be used of a belfry at Acre by one of the chroniclers of the Third Crusade, while a great tower filled with archers and crossbowmen at Kenilworth in 1265 was known as a 'bear'. The bore, picking holes in the masonry, is often called a 'mouse', and a common nickname for a prized stone-throwing engine is *Malvoisin* or 'Bad Neighbour', as Prince Louis named the great *petraria* which he sent for from France before beginning the siege of Dover in 1216.

The principal defence of the castle against the formidable resources of medieval siege-craft was, of course, in the strength of its own fortifications, expressly designed and developed to resist and overcome them. The direct answer to the pounding of the *petrariae* was the prodigious breadth of masonry which is such a feature of medieval military architecture, and the massive strength of the tower keep in particular was almost impervious to them, as King John found at Rochester in 1215. The plinth upon which the keep usually stands (12), and the similar plinths, batters and spurs at the base of other towers and walls (26), are sufficiently explained by the threat of the battering-ram, though they also served to make stones and other missiles dropped from above bound, splinter and ricochet among the assailants. The general transition from the rectangular to the curved or cylindrical tower towards the close of the twelfth century finds its explanation in the attentions in particular of the bore, which concentrated upon sharp angles, though to some extent also it represents an attempt to deflect the hurtling rocks from mangonel and trebuchet. The fact that the besiegers so often concentrated their resources upon the castle gate emphasises further the necessity of that continued elaboration of the gatehouse which in earlier chapters we have seen to be a feature of English medieval military architecture in all periods. The importance of the castle moat, wet or dry but preferably wet and as broad as possible, against all forms of attack is self-evident. Half the art of castle defence in an age of comparatively short-range weapons lay, indeed, in preventing the enemy from coming to close quarters, and the importance of many and well-placed firing apertures, of battlements and crenellation, and the overhanging hoarding or stone machicolation, in this respect again needs no further comment. But perhaps more than anything else some acquaintance with siege-craft emphasises anew the vital importance of the mural flanking towers in the great, fully developed stone castles of the later thirteenth century—towers thrust forward towards the field to cover the base of the walls against all the machinations of ram and bore, over-topping the walls to guard against attacks by escalade or belfry, and dividing them into defensible sections should such attacks bring some initial success.

The task of manning the castle's defences, of course, fell upon the garrison. At an early period after the Conquest all or part of the man-power required was at many castles provided by feudal means. Tenants of the lord of the castle were allotted the service of castle-guard or garrison duty in return for the lands they held of him, and at some of the greater castles especially, as at Dover, Windsor or Richmond, widespread and elaborate arrangements of this sort were made. But the feudal provision of garrisons had many disadvantages, and it is unlikely that the feudal resources of the kingdom were ever adequate to garrison all the castles within it. However this may be, it is certain that, by the second half of the twelfth century at least, feudal obligations of castle service, though they might still be demanded in war, were frequently commuted for a money rent, and that the hiring of soldiers as and when required was the most common method of garrisoning castles.

However provided, the numbers of the garrison of course vary in accordance with circumstances. Medieval chroniclers are notoriously unreliable on figures, but for what it is worth there is general agreement among them that the garrison of Rochester (9), which held out with such determination against King John in 1215, contained some hundred knights and men-at-arms apart from the lesser men. The garrison at Dover (36) under Hubert de Burgh a year later, when the castle was held for King John against the French Prince Louis, is said by Wendover to have included a hundred and forty knights and many men-at-arms. On the other hand the heroic defence of Odiham in Hampshire for a fortnight in the same wars is said to have been conducted by three knights and ten men-at-arms only. Turning to the records of about the same time, the Pipe Roll of 1174 mentions only twenty knights at Orford (11) and ten knights and forty men-at-arms at Wark in that year of rebellion against King Henry II by his sons. In the disturbances of 1193, when Count John was in rebellion against the government of Richard I, then a prisoner in Germany, the Pipe Roll gives a total garrison of seventy-five at both Norwich and Canterbury, made up of knights and men-at-arms both horsed and foot. After the fall of the

Bigod castle of Framlingham (16) to King John in the spring of 1216, the royal records mention some fifty-seven members of the rebel garrison, including twenty-six knights, twenty men-at-arms, seven crossbowmen and a chaplain. Some of the numbers given by the chroniclers may be exaggerated; the figures from the records may be for a variety of reasons incomplete; and all these examples are drawn from a limited period for which information is available. But in general it is safe to say that in the twelfth and thirteenth centuries at least, when the castle was at the height of its military importance, the numbers of the garrison were quite small, and the military importance of the castle was out of all proportion to the number of men within it.

The commanding officer of the garrison was usually the constable, to whom the custody of the castle was entrusted. On the whole it is not common to find the lord of the castle present at time of siege, partly perhaps because it was thought more honourable to fight in the field, and partly for somewhat less honourable reasons. To be besieged meant not only to be most uncomfortably cut off from the great world of events for possibly a long period, but might also end in disastrous expense, for the capture of a magnate usually entailed the payment of a heavy ransom as the price of release. After the constable himself, the leading members of the garrison were the knights. From their social status, their remuneration and their small number in relation to the rest of the garrison, we may conclude that they served as the officers of the little company. Beneath them came the more numerous body of men-at-arms, both horsed and foot. With and beneath them came archers and crossbowmen, smiths and farriers, watchmen and porters, carpenters and engineers, perhaps, to build and work stone-throwing engines, a chaplain who seems always to have been present, and the miscellaneous serving-men of a militant household. Amongst the names of those fined upon the Pipe Roll of 1176 for surrendering the castle of Appleby (p. 48) to the King of Scots in the recent war, and whose names may indicate their occupation, are William the clerk of Appleby (*clericus,* one in Orders), Rankil the miller, and Bernard the cook, the son of Wulfric.

Probably the most valuable members of the garrison for the defence of the castle were the crossbowmen. Condemned by the Second Lateran Council of the Church in 1139 as a weapon hateful to God, the crossbow was the most powerful and accurate hand weapon of the Middle Ages. Much employed by Richard on his Crusade and in his Continental campaigns, crossbowmen first appear extensively in English castles in John's reign. Thereafter, though late-thirteenth-century Carnarvon (22) was equipped for defence by the longbow, it is probable that the crossbow was never supplanted as the paramount weapon for castle defence, for though its rate of fire was slower than that of the longbow, its range was greater and it needed less space and less exposure for its discharge—while certainly neither weapon was ever seriously rivalled by the hand gun in the medieval period.

In addition to their personal arms, bow, sword, spear or axe, and the miscellaneous missiles dropped upon assailants too close to the walls, the garrison also made use of the artillery of mangonel, trebuchet and *ballista,* and with them of Greek Fire. Their targets were chiefly the siege-engines of their assailants, which they sought to shatter or burn before any great damage could be inflicted by them. Thus the Turks in the beleaguered city of Acre in 1191 succeeded in burning and destroying the engines of the King of France, which, we are told, so angered him that he fell sick. At Kenilworth in 1266 the garrison broke with their engines two great belfries which King Henry III and his son, the Lord Edward, caused to be erected, and each *petraria* of the royalists they answered with one of their own so that, according to one chronicler, the hurtling stones frequently met and shattered in mid-air. From the later twelfth century we find flat roofs covered with lead provided in castles, especially on keeps and towers, for *petrariae,* though there was always some danger of vibration weakening the masonry. Cannon in the later Middle Ages were an even greater threat in this respect and had also the disadvantage that they could not be dipped to fire down at the enemy. Nevertheless gun-ports make their appearance in English military architecture from the later decades of the fourteenth century, as at Bodiam (28) built in *c.* 1385, or the gatehouse at Carisbrooke (18) remodelled by Richard II in 1380, and it is worth noticing that cannon, like the earlier engines, were used as much for the defence of castles as for attacks upon them. On the whole, however, the introduction of gunpowder and cannon has left little mark upon the castle in this country: the bastion gun-emplacements on the north side of the Tower of London's outer wall are Tudor additions to the castle, and it is not until the mid-sixteenth century, when our period ends, that Henry VIII's coastal forts appear, designed specifically for defence by heavy guns.

The garrison in its defence did not rely only upon artillery to carry the war into the enemy's camp. It is noteworthy that in the account of the siege of Le Puiset in 1111 (p. 138) the garrison made a highly successful mounted sortie against the men of count Theobald, the king's ally. We have also noticed in an earlier chapter (pp. 69–70) how the great castles of the late thirteenth and early fourteenth centuries were often provided with more than one main gate in addition to lesser gates or posterns. Such developments in the design of the castle in fact made easier the tactics of aggressive defence common to all periods. Nor were such sorties merely the gallant last fling of desperate garrisons. At the siege of Kenilworth, for example, the garrison made repeatedly successful attacks upon the enemy's lines which caused much damage and loss of life among the royalists. The medieval garrison often contained a high proportion of cavalrymen, knights and horsed men-at-arms and crossbowmen capable of fighting on foot or on horseback, and the sortie provides one explanation of their presence—though not the only one, for we shall later see that the duties of the garrison were not confined to the defence of the castle.

Finally, in this analysis of the defence of the castle we must not omit perhaps the most vital factor of all, the adequate supply of provisions. Without that the strongest castle, though fully manned, must fall. Conversely, an attacking force, if its resources were sufficient for a close and prolonged investment, could always hope in the last resort to starve a garrison to surrender—as Prince Louis swore, but failed, to do at Dover in 1216. The chroniclers tell us that when in the autumn of 1215 the rebel barons decided to seize and hold Rochester against King John, those who undertook the defence were greatly worried by their inability to stock the castle adequately, and in the last desperate days some two months later imminent starvation helped to bring about the final capitulation. They were reduced, so the Barnwell annalist tells us, to horse-flesh and water, 'which bore hardly on those of them brought up in luxury'. (The garrison, in fact, under William de Albini of Belvoir, included some of the leading members of the baronial party.) In many another hard-pressed medieval siege failure of supplies is listed high by contemporary writers among the reasons for eventual surrender, as at Château-Gaillard in 1204 and Kenilworth in 1266. Surviving records accordingly show the extensive buying up of supplies to stock royal castles before the outbreak of hostilities. Corn is brought in in large quantities and often hand-mills are supplied to grind it within the castle, while the greater castles might have their own mills, like the tower wind-mill which Edward I built at Dover. Meat usually takes the form of pork or bacon, and salt is bought at the same time to preserve it. Sometimes, however, the meat may have been fresh, for eighty live cows (£16) and a hundred and thirty live sheep (£6 10s.) are brought into Lancaster Castle in 1215, perhaps to be slaughtered as required, and certainly the garrison of Bedford were keeping livestock in the outer bailey of the castle when it fell in 1224. Cheese and also beans were amongst the garrison's staple diet, and oats, in part at least for the horses, are supplied in large measure. The malt and barley sometimes mentioned may have been for beer, but the reading of medieval military accounts leaves a vivid impression of vast quantities of wine, then in England, as now in France, the staple drink of most classes of society. Arms are sometimes bought up, together with provisions, for the king's castles before the outbreak of hostilities, but not as a rule upon any large scale, presumably because they were either permanently stored in the fortress or were the personal equipment of the garrison. Miscellaneous stores appearing on the records include charcoal, firewood, iron, lead and tallow, and above all ropes, cords and cables, needed especially for *ballistae* and mangonels. It may be of interest, finally, to quote in translation, as one example of very many, the account for the stocking of Salisbury (1) in 1173, when that castle was put into a state of defence on the eve of the rebellion of the 'Young King' Henry Plantagenet against his father King Henry II. 'And in the stocking of Salisbury castle for 125 measures of corn £21 by the king's writ. And for 120 bacons £10 16s. 8d. And for 400 cheeses £8 by the same writ. And for 20 measures of beans 60s. by the same writ. And for 20 measures of salt 30s. by the same writ. And for 60 measures of malt £9 0s. 10d. by the same writ. And for iron 16s. by the same writ. And for charcoal

6*s*. 8*d*. by the king's writ. And for 4 hand-mills and their equipment 8*s*. by the same writ. And for 500 engines and 12 iron hooks and 1 chain for the bridge 13*s*. 4*d*. by the same writ. And for 1 large cord for the castle well 13*s*. 4*d*. by the same writ.'

To see the castle in action against the full concentrated resources of siege-craft, we can scarcely do better than to turn to the accounts written by well-informed contemporary chroniclers of the more important sieges and campaigns in the England of the twelfth and thirteenth centuries, when the military importance of the castle was at its height. Some of these accounts we have, of course, already drawn upon to supply examples for the analysis of siege-craft and counter-defences given above. The siege of Rochester castle in the autumn and early winter of 1215, conducted by King John against a baronial garrison, was the greatest single military event in the civil war which ended that king's reign and which also produced Magna Carta as an unsuccessful peace treaty. It is most notable, perhaps, as a striking example of the technique of mining, and also for the remarkable and possibly unique use which the gallant defenders made of the cross-wall with which the keep at Rochester, like most of the larger twelfth-century square keeps, was strengthened (p. 48). For when the king's miners brought down one corner of the great tower and the royalist forces poured in, the garrison continued their desperate resistance in the other half. 'For such was the construction of the keep', writes the knowledgeable chronicler of Barnwell, 'that a strong wall separated the half that had fallen from the other.' In all, the operation lasted for almost two months, from Sunday, 11th October, to the final surrender of 30th November, with the king present throughout, and was probably the greatest siege of a castle in England up to that date. The fall of Rochester had a severe effect upon the morale of the rebel party, and afterwards, says the same chronicler, 'few cared to put their trust in castles'. At the siege of Dover, held by Hubert de Burgh for King John in 1216 against Prince Louis of France, the ally of the rebel barons, mining was again intended to be the principal method of breaching the walls, and the most noteworthy feature of the action was the ambitious and elaborate plan conceived to carry it out. Commencing at a point well beyond the line of the outer walls, a great trench was aimed at the main gate which then stood at the north-west point of the fortifications. As the work went forward, the sappers threw up the earth from the trench so that they remained under cover from the defenders. Eventually the mine was well and truly sprung, and (as recent research has established) brought down one of the twin flanking towers of the gateway. Nevertheless, the defenders filled the breach with timber and the castle was not taken; but after the war, early in Henry III's reign, the shattered gateway was blocked up and heavily refortified, and a new main entrance made which is the present Constable's Gate.

The siege of Bedford Castle in 1224 we may describe in greater detail, for it provides a perfect example of a full-scale operation carried through to completion, and a wealth of contemporary written descriptions, supplemented by the evidence of official records, remain to provide information about it. The unhappy story of its lord, Fawkes de Bréauté, is one not unfamiliar in any age or country. A tried soldier, he had risen to great place chiefly by loyal and efficient service to King John in the civil wars that ended that king's reign. In the ensuing peace his power and high-handed habits accorded ill with the settled government which the new young king, Henry III, and his ministers sought to establish. Amongst the many rewards showered upon Fawkes by his late royal master had been Bedford Castle, previously confiscated from William de Beauchamp for his part in the rebellion against John. The tension created by Fawkes's persistent refusal to restore Bedford to its erstwhile lord, William de Beauchamp, at the mandate of a new and increasingly hostile government, was finally snapped when his castellans at Bedford seized and imprisoned in the castle a royal judge, Henry de Braybroke, proceeding on his lawful occasions through the district—occasions which included the hearing of suits at law directed against Fawkes de Bréauté himself. The act was outrageous. The young king, personally affronted by this insult to the hardwon dignity of the Crown, marched upon Bedford and concentrated about the castle the military array of the kingdom, supported by the Church militant in the person of the Archbishop of Canterbury and many of the clergy. The garrison, which was commanded by William de Bréauté, brother of the absent Fawkes, were solemnly excommunicated, and the secular arm of the state began the military operation by the raising of siege-engines. The chronicler of the nearby priory of Dunstable describes in detail their number, type and disposition. One *petraria* (probably in this instance a trebuchet) and two mangonels were set up on the east, two mangonels on the west which plied against the keep, and one mangonel on both the north and south sides of the castle. In addition, two strong and lofty belfries were raised to overlook the beleaguered fortress and filled with crossbowmen and look-outs (*exploratores*). By day and night the besieged had no rest from the showers of bolts and the thunderous pounding of the great stones against their walls and towers. For their part the garrison had no thought of surrender but, buoyed up by the hope that their lord Fawkes would bring relief to them, maintained a determined defence and inflicted considerable losses upon the royal forces. Ralph of Coggeshal tells us that a certain lord, Richard de Argentan, was seriously wounded in the stomach by a crossbow bolt which pierced his armour, that six other knights of the king's army were killed and over two hundred of the men-at-arms and labourers about the engines. With the arduous necessity of a prolonged siege and the mounting losses, bitterness grew, and King Henry swore that the garrison would be hanged if the castle were taken by storm.

Though unfortunately scarcely any trace of the fortifications of Bedford now remains to give substance to the story, the manner and methods of the castle's fall afford not only an excellent example of medieval siege-craft in action, but also an invaluable exposition of that 'one thing after another' system of defence, characteristic of the keep-and-bailey castle (*cf.* p. 62). Bedford was taken, the annalist of Dunstable tells us, in four main attacks. First the assailants captured the barbican or outwork, losing four or five men in the action. Next with heavier losses they stormed and took the outer bailey, and captured with it a great part of the garrison's equipment and provisions—horses and harness, hauberks, suits of mail and crossbows, livestock and corn. Now they were faced with their most formidable obstacles, the fortifications upon the mound itself, the ultimate stronghold of the casle. First their miners breached 'the wall next the old tower'—that is, it seems, the embattled wall round the summit of the mound, standing like a shell keep, but in this case encircling the tower keep, 'the old tower', which crowned the whole position.* This gaining of the inner bailey upon the mound was achieved only with great difficulty and further losses, and ten of the assailants who attempted to press home too ardently their victory were captured by the garrison and carried off into the last refuge of the keep. In the final act of the drama the miners again played the leading rôle. On the Vigil of

* The arrangement is found elsewhere. A cylindrical tower keep stands within a 'shell keep' on the mound at Launceston in Cornwall, and a similar combination once existed at Bungay in Suffolk.

the Assumption (14th August), towards Vespers, writes the chronicler, the mine beneath the keep was fired; smoke poured into the inner rooms where the defenders were gathered, the tower sank upon its foundations, great cracks appearing down its sides. Further resistance was impossible. The women, including Margaret, Fawkes's wife, and the prisoners, including Henry de Braybroke, the judge, were sent out, and the garrison hauled up the royal standard in token of their submission. The following morning, some eight weeks after the siege had begun, they came out before the king and, having been absolved from their excommunication, they, or the chief men among them, were hanged (42).

Surviving records in particular show the organisation and administrative effort which lie behind the drama of the siege of Bedford as the royal government mobilised its resources against the castle. They tell us of siege-engines carted from Lincoln and from Northampton and across Oxfordshire, while others were made on the spot by the many carpenters present. The constable of Windsor was ordered to provide horses for Master Thomas and his fellow carpenters together with their gear, 'so that they shall be able to travel to us by day and night as swiftly as they can and not tarry'. Master Henry the carpenter came from Lincoln and the sheriffs of London provided horses for Master Walter and Master Simon to ride to Bedford. Timber was sent from Northamptonshire, and the monks of Wardon complained of the losses they sustained when the king's men cut down trees from their woods. Ropes and cables for the engines came from London, from Cambridge and Southampton: hides to protect them from fire and to make slings for their throwing-arms were sent from Northampton: and tallow to lubricate them came from London again. To dig, fetch and shape the stones for the engines' bombardment a small army of labour was required, and the sheriffs of Bedfordshire and Northamptonshire were ordered 'without delay to cause to come to us at Bedford ... all the quarriers and stonecutters of your jurisdiction, with levers, sledges, mallets, wedges, and other of their necessary tools, to work stones for mangonels and *petrariae*'. Miners were sent from Hereford and the Forest of Dean by Roger de Clifford, constable of St. Briavel's, and amongst the company of them assembled at Bedford we may recognise, in Master Arnulf and William son of Lambert, two who had long served under King John. Amongst the crossbowmen we hear specifically of those coming from London, and orders went out for the supply by the thousand of quarells and bolts for their crossbows. Fifteen thousand were ordered up from Corfe Castle, and the bailiffs of Northampton were commanded, 'as you love us and our honour, that you cause to be made both by day and by night, by all the smiths of the town who are skilled in the art', four thousand quarells, well barbed and well flighted, to be sent with all speed to Bedford.

From the records, too, we catch some glimpse of the king's young majesty at war. His tents and pavilions were sent from London in good and strong carts, and we may surmise that they provided a colourful backcloth to the fighting, emblazoned with the royal arms and gay with fluttering pennants. His arms and his gear came also from London, and his personal requirements during the siege included large quantities of wine and the luxuries of almonds, pepper, saffron, ginger and cinnamon. At length, when all was over, the army was dismissed, the great engines dismantled and dispersed, some to Northampton and some to the Tower of London, and the king's arms and baggage were returned also to London in charge of Nicholas of the chamber. The castle of Bedford was razed to the ground, and Fawkes de Bréauté, deserted even by his wife, went into exile, to die a few years later still angrily uncomprehending the apparent injustice which turned loyal service to one king into armed rebellion against his successor.

Perhaps the most remarkable thing about the siege of Bedford in 1224 is that the castle, before it fell, held out for some eight weeks against the concentrated military resources of the whole kingdom. It is even more remarkable that in 1266 the castle of Kenilworth successfully withstood a similar concentration for no less than six months, and in the end was not taken but surrendered only upon terms. No two facts could demonstrate more clearly the strength of the medieval stone castle and the supremacy of defence over attack which it established. The siege of Kenilworth itself has all the romantic appeal of a lost cause. The castle was held by a desperately gallant band of the last supporters of earl Simon de Montfort after his defeat and death at Evesham. The siege was begun in earnest by Henry III and the Lord Edward, his son, with all the power they could raise, early in June 1266. The castle was still unbroken six months later, when in mid-December 'the emaciated garrison dragged its way out of its battered and stinking strongholds' (Professor Sir Maurice Powicke). Considerations of space prevent the full story of the action from being told here, but we must notice one or two salient facts about it. First, the fact that the castle was never taken by force may be bracketed with the fact that its broad water defences made impossible mining operations against it, for we may be sure that the two are not merely coincidental. Secondly, it is important to notice the manner of its final surrender. By October, though the hopes of relief from outside, which had borne them up throughout the long summer, had not entirely waned, the garrison's condition, especially by the lack of food and supplies, was becoming desperate. They therefore sought and obtained from their assailants a truce whereby, if no help came within forty

164

days, they would surrender. On December 14th, when the term was up and no relief forthcoming, they accordingly yielded up the castle and were allowed to march out with the honours of war.

The final surrender of Kenilworth upon terms is as important to us as any account of the conduct of the siege itself. For it is probable that the majority of medieval sieges were abandoned on the initiative of one side or the other, and after a much shorter struggle than that at Kenilworth, and that sieges or assaults carried through to the bitter end after the manner of Bedford or Rochester, or even Le Puiset, are the exception rather than the rule. One of the most valuable contemporary accounts of early medieval warfare is contained in the metrical chronicle of Jordan Fantosme describing the rebellion against Henry II in 1173–4. Jordan's account of the invasion of the north of England by William the Lion, King of Scotland, is especially instructive for the study of castle warfare.

When William the Lion crossed the Border in 1173 he came first to the castle of Wark, and there he demanded of Roger de Stuteville the constable,

'how he would act,
Whether he would hold it or surrender it—which course he
    would pursue.'

In the event the outcome was a compromise; Roger asked for, and was granted, a truce of forty days during which he would seek aid. Thus satisfied, the Scots moved off to Alnwick, the castle of Eustace de Vesci; but this again they did not take—though whether because they thought it too strong, or because another truce was obtained, we are not told. Next they marched against Warkworth and took it, though, be it noted, with little difficulty since the castle's defences were weak. From Warkworth the host proceeded to Newcastle upon Tyne, and here we are specifically told that no attack was launched because they lacked the necessary siege-train—even though the Pipe Rolls show that the great keep at Newcastle was not then completed.

> 'Well sees the king of Scotland that he will never complete
> The conquest of Newcastle-on-Tyne without siege engines.'

From Newcastle William the Lion marched upon Carlisle, held for the King of England by Robert de Vaux, and here the castle was invested.

> 'The swords resound and the steel clashes:
> Scarcely a hauberk or helmet there remained whole.'

But before the issue could be decided the siege was raised on the news that an English army under Richard de Luci, the Justiciar, was marching north, and the Scots withdrew into their own country.

It was not until the Easter of the next year, 1174, that the Scots marched south again. As before, they came first to Wark, but this time laid siege to it. The first assault on the castle failed, and William called up his siege-engines—which, profiting perhaps by last year's experience, he had brought with him—and ordered them to play upon the gate. They too failed, one of them grievously misfiring and striking down one of the Scottish knights.

> 'Then said King William: "Let us leave this siege:
> I see my men destroyed, and evil which cuts us off …
> … Roger d'Estuteville has proved our match".'

So the host moved off, the triumphant garrison but discreetly rejoicing, for Roger de Stuteville, the constable, forbade them to jeer ('Say nothing abusive: for God's sake let be!'), presumably in case the Scots should be shamed into renewing the attack. From Wark the host came again to Carlisle, but Robert de Vaux refusing to surrender to them, they withdrew and took the two castles of Appleby (p. 48) and Brough, the first with ease, the second after a stiff but not prolonged fight. From thence the Scots marched back upon Carlisle, where this time Robert de Vaux, both alarmed by the fall of Appleby and Brough and encouraged by rumours of his lord King Henry's return to England from France to deal with the situation, obtained a truce for fifteen days, at the end of which, if not relieved, he would yield up his charge. Thus leaving Carlisle, the host marched east upon Prudhoe which they vigorously assaulted. The castle, however, was well provisioned and stoutly defended, while Odinel de Umfraville, its lord, rode through the country raising a force for its relief:

'on maned Bauçan*...
... spurring continually day and night'.

After three days' unsuccessful effort before Prudhoe the siege was raised and, having divided his army, William the Lion himself marched upon Alnwick with a force of his French and Flemish allies. It was at Alnwick, before the castle, that they were attacked by the English army, led by Odinel de Umfraville amongst others, who came upon them unawares while the king, so Jordan Fantosme tells us, was at dinner with his helmet off. After a stiff fight they were defeated. William the Lion, his slaughtered horse pinning him to the ground, was captured and led away to imprisonment in Richmond castle, and the two-year Scottisch campaign in the north was over.

No doubt in his account of these events Jordan Fantosme may sacrifice some detail in the interests of poetic form and dramatic effect, and no doubt the Scottish army of 1173–4 was not notable for efficient organisation and was as much concerned with loot and rapine as with serious fighting. Yet, making these allowances, there remains to

* i.e. his horse, presumably piebald.

the modern ear a note of seeming casualness in the story of the campaign as Jordan tells it—and a note which is echoed in other accounts of other wars of the period. Of this seeming casualness it may be worthwhile to attempt some explanation. First, however, we must not exaggerate it. In Jordan's poem there is little support for the view still sometimes held of medieval warfare as a chivalrous tournament between high-minded and gentle knights. The Scots marched through the north with fire and sword. Richard de Luci, Justiciar of England, was heavy at heart as he rode through the once plentiful county of Northumberland,

'He rides in the ravaged and wasted country—
... Now it is in extreme famine; it is reduced to nothing',

and we are reminded of the grim advice on the proper conduct of war, given in the same poem by Philip, Count of Flanders, to the King of France:

'Thus should war be begun: such is my advice,
First destroy the land and then one's foes'.

Further, as regards the defence and capture of castles on which the campaign so largely turns, and in which our own interest particularly lies, it is well to remember that the aged constable, Gospatric son of Orm, and his garrison were heavily amerced later by the English king for their too facile surrender of Appleby to the Scots. Nevertheless, it does appear from this campaign that the full-scale and prolonged investment of a strong castle was something not lightly to be undertaken; that the yielding of a castle to a superior force by a garrison without hope of eventual success was not regarded as dishonourable; and that the compromise of some form of truce, often an agreement to surrender if no help came within a certain time, was frequently acceptable to both sides. When the keep was fired and the garrison of Brough surrendered, Jordan insists that they act honourably 'like knights':

'For they see very well that they will have no succour ...
... That is a right act which they do now.'

Before Roger de Stuteville at Wark decided to negotiate a truce with the Scots he begged of his chief men, 'Give me such advice that I may preserve my honour'.

For all this there were sound reasons which readily appealed to the hard-headed warriors of the Middle Ages. From the point of view of the assailants, the strong stone castle, well garrisoned and well provisioned, could not be taken without a full-scale and prolonged investment, perhaps degenerating into the deadlock of enforced and awaited starvation. To undertake this was a serious decision. Early medieval armies were small, and once committed to such an affair all other activities were sacrificed. Meanwhile, who could tell what might be happening elsewhere, or what chances might be missed? Once committed also, the army remained with reason acutely sensitive to attack from the rear, and news of the approach of a hostile relieving force was usually the signal for the siege to be raised. Nor was it easy to keep a medieval force long in the field and in one place. Feudal military service owed in return for land seems often to have been limited to forty days, while paid troops were both immensely expensive and liable to desert if long in arrears. Expensive, too, was all the paraphernalia of siege-trains and miners. It might well seem better, if a castle failed to yield to a first assault, to move on elsewhere, to indulge in profitable looting or by devastating the countryside to do as much easy harm as possible to the enemy. It may well be that such considerations in the end contributed to the decline of the castle's military importance; for when armies became bigger and the fear of assault from some neighbouring castle declined, it might be possible to mask or ignore the castles of an invaded countryside. But to revert: from the opposite point of view of the garrison, no castle, however strong and well defended, could hold out indefinitely, and in the last resort its resistance must be determined by the supplies of provender within it. Hence the hopes placed upon the advent of relieving forces, and hence meanwhile, not infrequently, the truce. The simile might not be too far-fetched which compared medieval castle warfare to a grim game of poker, bluff upon bluff—and often enough, if the truth be told, with wild cards and weapons concealed but ready for use.

These reflections may be wide of the mark, but they help to explain why so many medieval sieges were never pressed to a fighting conclusion. In fact, we know too little about medieval warfare, and especially the theories and principles behind it, which, if known, might throw new light upon the course of recorded events. To return once more to the sieges of Bedford and Kenilworth, for example, we may finally compare the manner of their ending. Bedford was eventually taken by storm and the garrison were hanged. The garrison of Kenilworth, who had given far greater trouble to the royal forces besieging them, eventually agreed to a truce, and when the term was up were allowed to withdraw with honour. It may be that these contrasting events reflect established contemporary practice, and that a garrison refusing all offers of terms could expect in the end no quarter. (Listen again to Jordan Fantosme, as the Scots march against Brough, swearing that, 'If it is not surrendered to them, no one shall go out of it alive'.) If so, the fact can be of wider interest. Rochester, too, in 1215 was taken by storm, and some of the chroniclers tell us that John intended to hang all the garrison until he was dissuaded by some of his captains, on the grounds that the same policy might be used against defeated royal garrisons

170

with harmful effects to general morale. The story has been used as one more nail in the coffin of John's reputation, yet, if later events at Bedford and Kenilworth are significant, it seems that the king's first thoughts were in accordance with contemporary customs of warfare.

We have spent much time upon sieges and the defence of castles, for defence was their basic rôle for which they were above all else designed. But it is important to remember that at all times the castle was also a firm base for agressive action. It is this fact which chiefly explains the high proportion of mounted men amongst the garrison which we have previously observed. Based upon the castle, and more or less secure within it from all but a full-scale attack, the small force of the garrison could command the surrounding countryside, riding out at will to protect and enforce the loyalty of neighbouring districts, to devastate the lands of their enemies, or to launch attacks on marauding and hostile forces. Thus, to take but a few examples, the knights of the rebel garrison of Leicester in 1174 attacked and plundered the town of Northampton and worked great damage upon the burgesses before returning in triumph to their own castle. In a letter patent dated 21st November, 1215, given at Rochester during the siege, King John ordered the Lady Nichola de la Haye—hereditary custodian of Lincoln, whose sex did not prevent her from heroically defending her charge against the rebels at a later date—to receive into her castle a force commanded by Geoffrey de Neville and Fawkes de Bréauté, sent there to harry the king's enemies. A little later in the same year the royal garrison from the recently captured Rochester rode out and took the neighbouring castle of Tonbridge in the lordship of the Clare earl of Hertford, then amongst the rebels. Again, when in 1216 Prince Louis, the ally of the rebels, gave to Gilbert de Gant the earldom of Lincoln, he gave him also the special task of suppressing the royal garrisons of Nottingham and Newark, who were destroying baronial houses and property in the district and seizing their lands for their own use. Edward I raised his great Welsh fortresses to hold down his new conquest of Wales, not as strongholds merely but as the active centres of military power.

Medieval castles had, of course, yet other military uses. They were valuable as havens and halting-places for field forces not specifically based upon them, while, in moments of crisis at least, their garrisons could be drawn upon to raise armies for the field. Roger of Wendover tells us that when in 1216 John wished to make a diversion to relieve Dover and Windsor, both then besieged, he raised a large force from his garrisons and proceeded to devastate the lands of the leading rebel magnates in East Anglia. (The plan worked and the siege of Windsor at least was raised.) Royal letters probably referring to this occasion, enrolled upon the surviving Patent Roll, are addressed to eleven loyal constables commending them to be ready, 'from dusk to dawn', with horses and arms to ride on the instant with a part of their garrisons to wherever Fawkes de Bréauté shall tell them on the king's behalf. The castle, too, was not infrequently a storehouse of munitions of war, as we saw Henry III drawing quarells from Corfe for the siege of Bedford and returning some of his engines to the Tower of London after the castle had fallen. Yet these are but secondary uses. It is the aggressive rôle of the castle combined with its defensive strength that chiefly explain its military importance. In war the two were complementary; the castle needed its strength to ward off the attacks which its value as an active centre of military operations invited. In the last resorts the land could be neither won nor held without the castles, and the castle dominated the warfare of the earlier Middle Ages because it dominated the land.

8

The Castle in Peace

Though designed pre-eminently for defence, the castle played its part in peace no less than war. First, it was, from the beginning, a residence as well as a fortress, and the combination of these two basic rôles is, indeed, the key to its whole history and development. In this combination the castle did no more than reflect the society which built, maintained and used it. For the Norman kingdom of England itself was founded by conquest; our medieval kings were, ideally and often in practice, warrior kings; and the aristocracy of which they were the head was predominantly a military aristocracy. We are seldom brought closer to this small but immensely powerful group of men than by their seals, and upon their seals, which they used in lieu of signatures to authenticate their documents, they portrayed themselves as they liked best to be thought of, armed cap-à-pie, mounted and charging home with brandished sword (38, 39). Or, again, in the churches, the armoured effigies and brasses upon their tombs yet bear witness to the overwhelming military traditions of the ruling classes in medieval England (40). For the members of this society, though they had their more or less unfortified houses and hunting lodges, the castle seems the proper setting, and indeed, though in the earlier period it was in brute fact the embodiment of their military and therefore their political power, we may suspect that throughout the Middle Ages, and certainly towards the end, prestige and convention contributed towards their choice of the castle as their principal residence.

There is another general feature of this medieval high

society which we must notice before discussing the castle as its residence. The members of it were almost continually on the move. The king himself, especially in the earlier Middle Ages, moved ceaselessly about his realm, visiting every region, seldom lying more than a few nights in one place, riding day by day and year by year the great circuit of the southern and midland counties, and ever and again pressing into the west and far north. And with him went not only a small army of servants, huntsmen and armed retainers, but also many of his barons, turn and turn about, with their followings, and many of the great officers of state with their own households and their clerks. For the king not only ruled but governed, and where he was there were also the court and the central government. In process of time, as the administration of government became more complex, the greater departments of state 'went out of court' and settled permanently in London, and eventually towards the end of our period the king came to rest there also. But the royal itinerary long remained an essential feature of medieval monarchy, and indeed lingered on to provide one explanation of the notorious predilection of Queen Elizabeth I for sleeping in strange beds, for in fact the great queen was amongst the last of our monarchs to live somewhat as her forebears had done. The medieval magnates of Church and State, when they were not with the king, moved similarly in their own spheres, from manor to manor through their own widely scattered estates, conducting their own widespread affairs. It is salutary to remember that medieval England was full of movement, and its roads and rivers constantly bearing the traffic of great households composed of men and women drawn from a variety of social levels. Though we may feel appalled by the physical discomforts of such journeying, partly imposed by the economic necessity of consuming the supplies from estates and manors where they stood, it had the supreme advantage of

174

making possible the personal control of affairs. The royal itinerary in particular made the personal government of the king a real and effective business, bringing him perhaps closer to his subjects than our monarchs have ever been until this present age. And amidst the detailed knowledge of their kingdoms which medieval kings thus gained, we may count a shrewd knowledge of their castles, upon which their itinerary was largely based, and upon which depended, in the last resort, the security of their realm.

Of the two basic rôles of the castle as residence and fortress, we have already seen that the former eventually triumphed as the military importance of the castle declined from the late fourteenth century onwards. But the 'domestication' of the castle in the later Middle Ages, which we have already examined from the architectural point of view in an earlier chapter, only emphasised its residential character, which became more obvious and more luxurious as its defences were lowered. It is noteworthy that the twelfth-century description of Ardres, already quoted (pp. 30–1) concentrates more upon the wonderful amenities of the timber house upon the mound, with its chambers great and small, its private room where they sometimes had a fire, its kitchen, its *loggia,* and its chapel 'like unto the tabernacle of Solomon in its ceiling and painting', than upon the military strength of the castle. At about the same time, Gerald of Wales, churchman, courtier and man of letters writing of his own family's castle of Manorbier in Pembrokeshire, describes it proudly in terms reminiscent of a modern advertisement for a gentleman's country seat—which indeed in a contemporary sense it was. 'The castle called Maenor Pyrr', he writes, '... is distant about three miles from Penbroch. It is excellently well defended by turrets and bulwarks, and is situated on the summit of a hill extending on the western side towards the seaport, having on the northern and southern sides a fine fish-pond under its walls, as conspicuous for its grand appearance as for the depth of its waters, and a beautiful orchard on the same side, enclosed on one part by a vineyard, and on the other by a wood, remarkable for the projection of its rocks, and the height of its hazel trees. On the right hand of the promontory, between the castle and the church, near the site of a very large lake and mill, a rivulet of never-failing water flows through a valley, rendered sandy by the violence of the winds. Towards the west, the Severn sea, bending its course to Ireland, enters a hollow bay at some distance from the castle.'

Gerald's description of his beloved Manorbier sheds a calm light upon the castle even of this early period, and pleasantly reminds us that it was indeed a residence no less than a fortress. As soon as written administrative records become at all common from the mid-twelfth century, we can learn from them how much attention contemporaries paid to the domestic quarters within their castles, see something of what those quarters were like, and catch glimpses also of the life led within them. Thus the Pipe Rolls show that as early as the reign of Henry II (1154–89) certain of the royal castles most favoured as residences were already becoming palaces within, however heavily fortified without. At Windsor (37) Henry built in stone, on the north side of the upper bailey where the cliff behind it made it most secure from attack, a new royal lodging, as well as enclosing the bailey with a new and towered stone wall. Within the shell keep upon the mound, also, there were further residential buildings including a hall and chambers in stone, and others again within the lower bailey. Though the rolls provide all too few details, we hear in particular of the king's hall at Windsor, of his chambers, his larder, kitchen and almonry, of the repair of the seats of the king and queen in the chapel, of pictures sent from London to the castle, and, a little later, of a certain garden within it. In

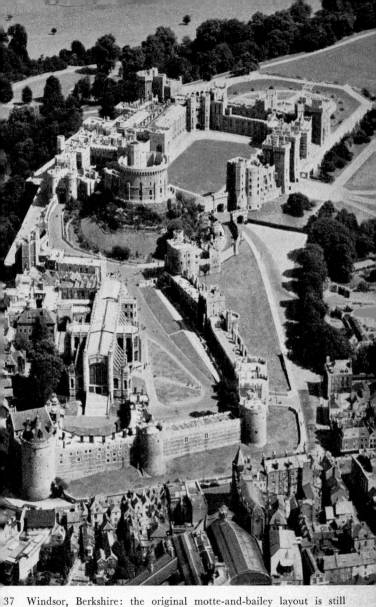

37 Windsor, Berkshire: the original motte-and-bailey layout is still clearly apparent beneath the accumulated stonework of succeeding centuries

38   Seal of John de Warenne,
Earl of Surrey, 1231–1304
(From the Public Record
Office, Barons' Letter)

39   Seal of Henry de Percy,
Lord of Leconfield, Top-
cliffe and Petworth, *d.*
1314 (From the Public
Record Office, Barons'
Letter)

40   Tomb of Robert Courthouse, Duke of Normandy (*d.* 1134) in
Gloucester Cathedral

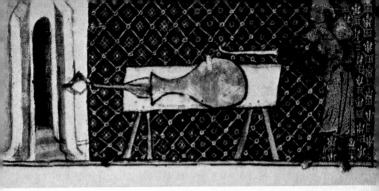

41 The earliest known illustration of a cannon, 1326 (From the Walter de Milemetes MS. 92 at Christ Church, Oxford)

42 The end of the siege of Bedford in 1224 (From the Parker Matthew Paris, *Chronica Majora*, MS. 16 at Corpus Christi College, Cambridge)

CASTLE CHAPELS

45 Ludlow, Shropshire: the twelfth-century chapel

46　Licence of Edward I to Stephen de Penchester and Margaret his
wife to fortify the castle of Allington in Kent (1281) (see p. 199)
(Public Record Office, E 359/470)

47　Allington, Kent (*c.* 1281)

48 Oakham, Rutland: the twelfth-century hall

49 Winchester, Hampshire: the mainly thirteenth-century hall

all, so far as we are able to compute it, it is probable that about a third of the total heavy building expenditure upon Windsor in Henry's reign was devoted to its residential quarters—and this, it may be noted, at a time when the English castle was at the height of its military importance.

At Winchester at the same time the Pipe Rolls, amongst continuous entries of building expenditure, tell us of the king's hall within the castle and of hedges set about it, of work upon the castle chapel of St. Judoc, upon the kitchens and upon a 'house' for the king's falcons, of work in painting the king's chamber and in preparing a separate chapel for the 'Young Queen', the wife of Henry's eldest son who was crowned in his father's lifetime. At Nottingham, again, much of the heavy expenditure by Henry II was devoted to the residential quarters within the castle. A new great hall was built between 1180 and 1183, private chambers were raised, the tower keep itself was given new timber flooring, and we hear also of an almonry, a mews for falcons, a garden and the park attached to the castle. It may be that this work was intended chiefly for Count John, the king's beloved youngest son, to whom, Hoveden tells us, he had granted the castle in 1174. But the Pipe Rolls of the later twelfth century are full of references to the royal lodgings within the castles, built, repaired and set in order, up and down the land and in places as far apart as Exeter and Carlisle, against the king's coming as he moved constantly through his realm. And life within the castle, after the day's journey or the chase, must have been pleasant enough, and by no means devoid of comfort. King Henry in his last years caused a garden to be made before his chamber window at Arundel, a castle then in his hands, and King John, who followed his father's example in providing in his castles dwellings fit for kings, commanded new kitchens to be built at Ludgershall and Marlborough with ovens big enough to roast two or three oxen in each.

For the reign of Henry III (1216–72), which extends over the greater part of the thirteenth century, a new series of records, the *Liberate* Rolls,* set out, in far greater detail than the Pipe Rolls, the expenditure of one of the most fastidious of our kings, living in an age which represents the high-water mark of medieval civilisation. Amongst the wealth of information which these invaluable rolls contain concerning the king's works at his castles, we may concentrate first upon favoured Winchester, which provides an outstanding example of Henry's high standard of living in the middle years of the reign. A typical order to the sheriff of Hampshire, dated in December of the year 1250, orders him to cause to be painted the king's new chapel in his castle of Winchester with the story of Joseph, and to floor the same chapel with tiles; to paint the table by the king's bed with images of the guardians of Solomon's bed; to pave the chambers of the king and queen with tiles; to make wooden windows in the gallery of the queen's chapel; to repair the privy chamber before the door of the Jew's tower; and to repair the long chamber above the stable in the tower where the wardrobe is usually made. Elsewhere on the rolls for these years we hear of the great hall (49) —now all that remains of the castle, and owing its present gracious appearance to the taste of the same King Henry III—which is to be repaired and its cracks filled in, while the king's seat in the hall is to be repainted and so are the doors and the windows, and the pictures above the king's dais (where his table was placed at one end of the hall, as the High Table is still in college halls today) are to be renewed. Tables, chairs and forms are ordered for the chambers of the king and queen, and the queen's chamber is to

* They take their name from the writs of *liberate* which they enrol, i.e. orders to the Exchequer to pay out (Latin *liberare*) certain sums of money for purposes stated. The earlier rolls are printed in translated calendar form by H.M. Stationery Office.

be painted with green paint, new candlesticks to be supplied, and a 'Majesty' provided with gilded images about it for her devotions. Amongst the ever-increasing number of other private chambers in the castle, we hear of one for the king's stewards in the castle, to be conveniently built between the hall and the kitchen; of another vaulted chamber for the king's knights which is to be wainscoted; of chambers for the castle chaplain and priests; and of a new chamber to be made by the royal stables to contain three beds and the harness. And at Winchester in the reign of this devout king spiritual welfare was as lavishly provided for as creature comforts. A new private chapel (probably the new chapel ordered to be painted in the 1250 order to the sheriff cited above) is to be made by the king's bed, and for his main chapel a marble altar is provided. In the queen's chapel, behind which stood the castle dovecote, a beam was to be set up spanning the width, bearing a cross in the centre and figures of Mary and John on either side. The following year an order went out to paint on the westward gable in the same chapel an image of St. Christopher carrying Our Lord in his arms, as he is painted elsewhere, and an image of St. Edward the king, how he gave his ring to a pilgrim, to be painted in like manner.

Though Winchester may be exceptional in degree, the Liberate Rolls especially make it clear that in the course of the thirteenth century many other royal castles were receiving ever more elaborate residential quarters within the increasingly safe circuit of their walls. At Windsor, in the lower bailey, to the east of the existing hall now much improved, new royal lodging and a new chapel were raised, with a cloister between them, surrounding a lawn, and provided with a stone bench near the king's chamber. Meanwhile the lodgings in the upper bailey built by Henry II were extended and improved, and made over, apparently, to the especial use of the queen. In 1236 the queen's chamber there was set in order for Henry III's bride, the Lady Eleanor of Provence. Glass was set in two of the windows overlooking the garden, with shutters to open and shut, and another glass window, set in the gable, painted with the Tree of Jesse. The new queen, however, or possibly her husband, remained dissatisfied, and the following year the chamber was rebuilt. In 1239 Eleanor gave birth to her first-born son, the future Edward I, and a nursery was provided for him. The bailiff of Windsor later in the year was ordered 'to cause the chamber of our son Edward to be wainscoted, and iron bars to be made to each of the windows of the same chamber'. Subsequently, as the king's family increased, so the royal nurseries next the queen's apartments in the upper bailey at Windsor were extended.

At Ludgershall, again, to choose one example of many, the constable of the castle was ordered, in May 1244, to make a new hall there, sixty feet by forty, in place of the old, with four permanent windows, and at the end a pantry and a buttery; to build two kitchens, one for the king and one for his household (King John's kitchens with their great oven for two or three oxen being now apparently out of date); to wainscote the chambers of the king and queen; to repair the outer chambers; and to enclose the castle park with ditch and hedge all round. At the neighbouring Marlborough, a writ of 1241 to the constable ordered, amongst other things, a new devecote by the castle; a new glazed window before the door of the queen's chapel; a new fireplace in the cellar before the queen's chamber, the same cellar to be wainscoted and whitened and provided with a window painted with a dove and barred with iron; a portico to be made between the queen's chamber and her chapel, and a new door at the entry of her chamber; a new wardrobe good and large with stoves, behind the chapel of St. Nicholas; and a larder for the king in a suitable place. At Llantilio (White Castle, Monmouthshire) a new hall was provided with a pantry and buttery, and a new chapel at near-by Skenfrith, while at Salisbury a nurse's chamber was built. Everywhere fireplaces were fitted in, and chapels repaired, improved and given rich furnishings. And everywhere, too, there was colour; in the images and painted glass of chapels, and in the glass and painting of halls and chambers alike. The wainscoting of one of the queen's privy chambers at Windsor was to be painted 'of a green colour with gold stars', and in the same castle the cloister was to be decorated with pictures of the Apostles, under the supervision of Master William the king's painter, a monk of Westminster. At Hertford Castle the king's great chamber was to be wainscoted, whitened and diapered in colours. Even the Tower of London, like other towers in this and later centuries of the Middle Ages, was kept clean and white, in some contrast to its present appearance, by a liberal application of whitewash—from which indeed it gets its name, the White Tower.

With the decline of the castle's military importance from the fourteenth century onwards, its residential quarters expanded apace and its domestic comforts increased, very often at the expense of its military strength. There is no need to add much here to what has already been said of this process in an earlier chapter. There, we took Edward III's great works at Windsor, converting the fortress into a palace, to be in some measure symbolic of the increasing 'domestication' of the castle in the later Middle Ages, and here it may suffice if, remembering also his chapel and college of priests for his Order of the Garter in the lower bailey, we notice something of the composition of the new royal lodging which he built in the upper bailey. The great hall is now changed almost beyond recognition, but something of its original grandeur can be seen from Hollar's seventeenth-century engraving, showing its structural appearance much as Edward left it. In the royal apartments themselves, the king had a set of five chambers, with, in addition, a painted chamber, a great chamber, a chapel and a closet. His great chamber, used perhaps on more formal occasions, must have been very large, for it was provided with some twenty windows. The decoration of the Painted Chamber we do not know, but the colouring of 'the fifth chamber called la Rose' included azure and gold, green and vermilion. Edward's queen had a set of four chambers and a chapel, arranged about a cloister. One at least of her rooms was well supplied with mirrors, and another is pleasingly called her 'daunsyng chambre'. All the chambers of king and queen alike were upon the first floor, the ground floor, following the usual medieval practice, being used for storage and offices. The furnishings listed as supplied for the royal apartments are somewhat austere, benches and stools for seats, and trestle tables, but we may imagine them in the warm and colourful setting of wainscoting, hangings, coloured glass, bright painting and, in the winter, good fires.

In discussing the residential rôle of the castle we have, by the bias of the documentary evidence which survives, used chiefly royal examples. But the barons, no less than their liege lord, made their castles as comfortable as they could, and indeed since no one magnate could rival the king in the number of castles he possessed, must have spent much longer in them. We began by quoting the proud description by Gerald of Wales of the de Barri castle of Manorbier in its peaceful setting, and we may end with a quotation from a fifteenth-century Welsh manuscript, lyrically describing the desirable and unwarlike appurtenances of the great castle of Raglan (p. 95) in Monmouthshire, founded by Sir William ap Thomas, 'the Blue Knight of Gwent'. 'Perfect spheres and elegant pearls in clusters like grapes, the store of the Blue Knight; and about the palace there were orchards full of apple trees and plums and figs, and cherries and grapes, and French plums, and pears, and nuts, and every fruit that is sweet and delicious.'

We have spent some time upon the castle as the dwelling of the medieval aristocracy, not only because it was from the beginning a residence no less than a fortress, but also because this peaceful and domestic aspect of it, especially in the earlier period upon which we have chifly concentrated, is not always easy to realise. It requires an effort of the imagination to recall that, in all periods of the Middle Ages and not only towards the end of its history, the castle was lived in far more than it was fought in, and it comes as something of a surprise to read, even in records of the twelfth and thirteenth centuries, of gardens, cloisters, dovecotes and cowsheds within it, or vineyards (as at Windsor), well-stocked fishponds and parks without. Investigation of the castle as a residence, moreover, affords pleasing glimpses of the life inside it—a life which appears both grand and spartan at once, occasionally elegant, and sometimes enviable. Lost splendours are indeed evoked, and perhaps regretted, when we learn, for example, that in preparation for his Christmas at Winchester Castle in 1206 King John commanded the sheriff of Hampshire to procure one thousand five hundred chickens, five thousand eggs, twenty oxen, one hundred pigs and one hundred sheep; or when everywhere upon the records we meet the endless convoys of good wine rolling towards the royal castles. At the same time it must be emphasised that in the twelfth and thirteenth centuries at least, the provision by king and barons alike of very adequate residential quarters and amenities in and about the castle did not then impair its military efficiency. Henry III's close and tasteful attention to the lodgings within his castles coincides in time with the sweeping advances in military architecture during the thirteenth century which culminated in the impregnable achievement of Conway (21) or Beaumaris (24)—themselves luxuriously appointed within—and it was not until the later Middle Ages that comfort took priority over strength. The close juxtaposition of peace and war in the medieval castle may suggest both that even in that stern epoch war remained the exception to peace, and that the gulf between the two was not then so wide as it has since become. But however this may be, certainly at no time in its history was the castle filled only or always with the tramp and clatter of soldiers; the sound of revelry in the hall, the rustle of dresses in the chambers of the queen, or the laughter of children in the bailey, are as authentic an echo for our ears to strain after as shouts of battle and the clash of arms.

The fact that the medieval castle was lived in by no means exhausts the list of its non-military uses. The study of the castle in the institutional sense of what it was *for* has not as yet gone very far, but we are beginning to know some of the uses made of it in the thirteenth century, and there is good reason to suppose that they may stand for both earlier and later periods, for they follow on naturally from the castle's two basic rôles as residence and fortress. Thus the fact that castles were the residences of the great ones of the land, and more permanently of their officials, made them almost inevitably the centres of local government and of the power they symbolised. The baronical castle commonly stood as the focal point of widely scattered estates and franchises, the head, as the contemporary phrase ran, of the lord's honour, while the king's castles either similarly stood at the head of estates or districts, or, more commonly, were in the custody of sheriffs, the chief local officials of the Crown, and thus became the centres of country admin-istration. It was in the castle, in the hall, that often the local courts of shire, hundred or honour were held, to the castle that a man repaired to plead his suit, present his services or pay his taxes, and through its gates, watched by the porter, passed a stream of litigants and supplicants, tenants and bailiffs, tax-collectors and messengers, intent upon their daily business. There were other miscellaneous affairs of a paternal and pious authority too, as when King Henry III ordered his constable of Windsor, in 1241, 'to cause the hall of our castle of Windsor, and also the hall within the tower [i.e. the keep] of the same castle, to be filled with poor folk on Good Friday and to feed them'. We may be sure that the 'chamber of the clerks' which was built in Nottingham castle in 1186 long remained a busy place as the king's writs came in and were returned, juries were empanelled, and rolls and vouchers of dues, payments and pending cases made up.

Residence of kings and magnates and their officials, the centre of local government and affairs, the castle was also, again by virtue chiefly of its strength, sometimes a treasury, sometimes an armoury (as the Tower still is) and, almost invariably, a prison. We may perhaps end this chapter with some notice of only the last of these subsidiary uses, the long-continued rôle of prison, for it is this which has contributed more than anything, perhaps unjustly yet not without cause, to the romantic notoriety of the castle—and in so doing, as we have seen, has also changed the word 'donjon' meaning keep into the more modern 'dungeon', with all its connotations of uncomfortable incarceration. Medieval records are full of references to the castle gaol, and in places resound also with complaints, true or false, of unjust imprisonments and other misdemeanours by the constable who was in charge of it. He indeed seems at times to have been, by modern standards, high-handed in his acts, and we read of a constable of Banbury (a castle then belonging to the Bishop of Lincoln) who, pursuing an escaped prisoner, caught and executed him on the spot. No doubt he had some provocation, for we know that the heaviest fines could be imposed upon those who allowed their prisoners to escape. One would not imagine escape to have been easy, though a letter of King John in 1203 contains what is apparently an interesting reference to a prison riot. The king, having ordered the constable of Corfe to send him two of his prisoners, Savaric de Malleon and Amery de Forz, under good escort, adds that he is to take care that a sufficient garrison remains to guard the castle with the rest of its prisoners, 'better than it was guarded when the aforesaid Savaric took and held the keep against us'. As for the castle prisoners themselves, they included not only local offenders but also high-placed political prisoners of state, and amongst the latter there are some whose lot was tragic enough to justify the castle's grim reputation in this respect. The unhappy Eleanor, sister of that Prince Arthur whom King John stands accused of murdering for his claims to the English throne, languished forty years in Bristol castle before her death in 1241. All contemporary chroniclers agree that the same king caused the wife, son and daughter-in-law of his fallen companion William de Braose to be barbarically starved to death in Windsor castle, and Berkeley castle in Gloucestershire witnessed the atrocious murder, in 1327, of one of the most illustrious of political prisoners, the deposed King Edward II:

'The shrieks of death, thro' Berkeley's roofs that ring,
Shrieks of an agonising King!'

There was a dark strand in medieval life, inextricably interwoven with its piety, its shrewdness, its chivalry and its humour, and the castle was sometimes the scene not only of good living and administrative efficiency, but also of brutality, and saw life taken by means less honourable than war.

9

The Castle in General

In the last few chapters, having first said something of *how* the castle was built, we have endeavoured also to show *why* it was built by discussing its uses both in war and peace. In so doing we have broken out of the conventional confines of most books on castles with their too exclusive concentration upon mere architectural description. There yet remain for this last chapter some general points and reflections upon the whole subject of the castle, to round off our sketch of this dominating feature of the English medieval landscape and to increase our understanding of its great importance in the life and society of the Middle Ages. And, finally, we must attempt to explain how it was that this importance eventually declined. But at the outset it must again be emphasised that so little work has yet been done upon the castle from any save the architectural point of view that any observations we may make will inevitably be more tentative than positive.

Until very recently no real attempt has been made to estimate the number of medieval castles in the realm, and no full list of them has ever been compiled. In practice, of course, such a task is extremely difficult by reason both of the amount and the deficiencies of the evidence, whether archaeological or written, and complicated also by the fact that the number of castles varies from one century to another. However, it now seems established that from written evidence alone some three hundred and fifty castles are known to have been in use in England and Wales about the year 1200. Bearing in mind the deficiencies of this written evidence, therefore, we can probably take four hundred as a safe notional figure for the total number of castles in use in that area at that date. Next, from the vantage point of this more or less firm ground we can look both forward and backward. First, impressive as the figure of four hundred is, it represents without doubt a falling off from the total figure of, say, the year 1150. Though that total is not and probably never will be known, we can be fairly certain that the first half of the twelfth century saw the greatest number of castles that were ever in England, for then to the extensive foundations of the decades immediately following the Norman Conquest were added the many strongholds—often, it is true, of a minor order—which the civil wars of Stephen's reign brought forth. Thereafter the number of castles was rapidly reduced. The advent of peace in 1153 was followed by the destruction of the 'adulterine', or new, unlicensed strongholds of the Anarchy, and the new king, Henry II, both effectively controlled new private fortification and began a settled policy of making the demolition of baronial castles, where possible, the penalty of rebellion, or even of suspected disloyalty. Further, and perhaps most important of all, the heavy cost of building in stone both prevented new castles from being raised with the ready ease of the past, and led also to the abandonment of many existing sites whose owners could not afford to fortify them after the new fashion. Thus we come again to the total of four hundred castles about the year 1200, and looking forward we may perhaps surmise, though with less confidence, that this figure remains roughly constant for the next two centuries, until the declining military importance of the castle began the long and final process of further reduction in its numbers. Though new castles were raised, they were, as we have stressed in earlier chapters, exceptional in being new castles, and it is at least probable that their number did no more than offset the number of existing castles then abandoned or destroyed by the circumstance of war and politics or the waning fortunes of their lords.

The distribution of these hundreds of castles is also full of interest. They are to some extent inevitably concentrated on the borders of the medieval kingdom, in the far north towards Scotland, along the south-eastern coast towards the Continent, and especially in the broad district of the Welsh Marches. But one of the most striking facts about them is that they are also found in great number all over the interior and in every county however far removed from any possibility of war against an external enemy. In this wide, comprehensive distribution they again reflect the society they served. The English medieval castles were many of them founded by the Norman conquerors to hold down conquests won, and were thereafter maintained and augmented in an age in which power might be physically asserted or resisted and possessions might need to be defended in arms—when warfare, in short, was as likely to be waged in the interior as on the frontiers. If on the one hand they represent an impressive effort to achieve internal security, they bear witness on the other to the continual possibility of civil faction.

In fact, of course, the distribution of castles in the Middle Ages was not, and could not have been, the result of any unified policy imposed from above in the national interests, whether of defence, expansion or internal security. Indeed the basic geographical knowledge was not available for such strategic planning from the centre even had the political and economic structure of the kingdom made it conceivable. The distribution of medieval castles is tactical rather than strategic, determined by many and sometimes conflicting interests, and is the arbitrary result of local needs and circumstances. It reflects above all the distribution of lands and power among the barons and the king, and though the king's lands and interests were wide enough for him to think in terms of the whole state, the royal

189

castles were nevertheless only a fraction of the total number. Thus even the thickly planted castles of the wide Welsh Marches were not units in a national plan against the long-suffering Welsh, but rather separate strongholds set to defend and extend the particular territory of their individual lords. Moreover, though within its local setting the actual site of the castle was usually chosen with skill from the military standpoint, and though it was often founded to guard a road or valley, river or crossing, or to defend a town—though the road may now be vanished, the river no longer navigable, the ford abandoned and the town shrunk to a village—its setting and position may not be the result of purely military considerations. A knowledgeable thirteenth-century chronicler thus describes King John's new castle of Odiham soon after it was built: 'A castle ... set in fair meadows and close to the woods which the king had caused to be built for his sport.' The manor of Odiham lay in good hunting country, and John in choosing it for his castle may well have been moved as much by the delights of the chase as by military necessity—though when the test came a few years later the castle was strong enough to be held, as Roger of Wendover tells us, for three days by a garrison of three knights an ten sergeants only.

So long as the castles retained their military importance, the whole question of their distribution and control was the very stuff of medieval politics, for the control of any district turned upon the possession of the castles which commanded it. In an earlier chapter we discussed the building of Orford (11) in Suffolk from the point of view of *how* it was done (p. 117). If we now ask *why* it was done we shall find one clear example of a castle founded as the result of political considerations. When, in 1154, Henry II ascended the throne there were no royal castles in Suffolk, and power in the county was dangerously concentrated in the hands of Hugh Bigod, earl of Norfolk, who held there the three castles of Framlingham, Bungay and Walton, with Thetford just on the Norfolk border. As early as 1157 Henry, upon some pretext now unknown, was able to confiscate all four Bigod castles, and also acquired Eye in Suffolk and Norwich in Norfolk, the latter the administrative centre of the two counties. Although in 1165 the king restored Framlingham and Bungay to the earl, Walton and Thetford he retained, and in the same year also began to build his new castle at Orford upon the coast not far from Framlingham—while the earl about the same time strengthened his castle at Bungay with a new tower keep. Orford was finished by 1173, and in that year a rebellion against the king broke out in which earl Hugh was one of the leaders and East Anglia one of the principal theatres of action. In view of the geographical position of the castle and the context of events, there can be little doubt that Orford was raised as part of a struggle for power between king and earl in which the control of Suffolk was the prize, just as these same events throw light on the motives which led Hugh Bigod to rebel. In his rebellion the earl was defeated, his castles of Framlingham and Bungay again confiscated, and this time demolished. In the first twenty years of the reign of Henry II, therefore, the political balance of power in terms of castles had been in Suffolk entirely reversed. It only remains to add that after the death of both King Henry and earl Hugh, Framlingham and Bungay were restored to the house of Bigod, and the former was rebuilt stronger than before (16) to become again the centre of rebellion against King John in 1216.

All history, it has been said, is local history. Certainly the fortunes of individual castles can often help to explain great political events, and much of the history of medieval England is locked up in its castles. The heresy which sees the political history of the Middle Ages as a simple conflict between the Crown on the one hand and the baronage on the other is obviously untenable, for such a situation would have made monarchy impossible. Medieval kings of necessity retained the support of most of their barons most of the time, while of the small but immensely powerful group of individuals who formed the medieval baronage, a varying but substantial proportion were bound to the king by ties of service and loyalty, reward and community of interest, and not infrequently by blood. Nevertheless, putting ourselves for a moment upon the throne, it was obviously in the king's interest to control private fortification by insisting upon licences for new works (46), to prevent the exclusive control of any district by baronial castles, to ensure so far as possible that the more important fortresses should not be in the hands of those he could not trust, to keep his own castles firmly in his own power, and in general to see that royal castles were placed where they were most necessary to impress and uphold the authority of the Crown. From the baronial point of view, on the other hand, castles it was desirable to possess and essential to retain. In an age in which political opposition not infrequently appealed to arms, the control of castles was likely to become a burning issue. There is the ring of truth in the simple account by a Welsh chronicler of the causes of the political crisis of 1215 which led to civil war and Magna Carta. The rebels, he writes, swore they would not make peace with the king until he restored the liberties of the church, 'and until he also restored to the good men of England and Wales their lands and the castles which he at his will had taken without either right or law'. In the event, amongst the barons who fought King John on this occasion were Clinton who had lost Kenilworth, Lacy who had lost Pontefract, Stuteville who had lost Knaresborough, and Fitz Walter, Mowbray and Mandeville who claimed by right the custodies of Hertford, York and the Tower of London respectively. Magna Carta itself, the Great Charter of English liberties, insisted in one of its most important clauses upon the restoration of private castles seized by the Crown without due processes of law.

The embodiment of military and therefore of political power, the residence of the great, the hub of administration and the centre in so many ways of medieval public and private life, affecting most ranks of society by its omnicompetence and the necessary service and labour of its maintenance—how then are we to explain the decline of the castle in the later Middle Ages? The chief reason appears to be the slow decline in its military importance from the late fourteenth century onwards, and the immediate cause of this in turn to be the changing character of warfare. In the military sphere we have already stressed that the introduction of gunpowder was only one amongst other changes, and not at first important as a challenge to the castle's supremacy. Far more important was a general change in the conduct of English warfare, which, waged by larger and more professional armies, became increasingly a matter of battles in the field, and turned in consequence less and less upon the castle. It may be also that within this wider change in the conduct of war, the castle, in the very perfection it had achieved by the end of the thirteenth century, contributed something to its own military decline. 'A castle like Caerphilly', wrote the late Professor Hamilton Thompson, 'did not put an end to local warfare: it merely warned an enemy off a forbidden track.' In other words, because the castle had become almost impregnable to all but the most elaborate and sustained attack, the enemy no longer attempted to take it, and the trial of strength was made elsewhere. It is significant in this respect that some of our greatest castles have no military history.

But such changes in the conduct of warfare themselves

require more explanation, and certainly the causes of the decline in the castle's importance go deeper. We saw in the first chapter of this book that the origins of the castle lie with the growth of feudal society, and it is usual to say that the decline of the castle reflects in turn the decline of feudalism in the later Middle Ages. But this convenient equation helps little without some further comment. The private castle was the symbol and embodiment of the power of the medieval aristocracy, yet in the later Middle Ages there is little obvious sign of this power decreasing, and in Tudor times the problem of the 'overmighty subject' was still bewailed and feared. Nor was the military power of the nobility much reduced by the undoubted decline of purely feudal obligations of military service, owed by their tenants in return for land; the newer system of fee-paying lordship and salaried service—known to historians as 'Bastard Feudalism'—gave them probably more power, with greater opportunities of more efficiently applying it. Further, a too close association of the rise and fall of the castle with the rise and fall of a strictly feudal lordship based on the tenure of land, somewhat begs the question of the royal castles, which stood always for something more than the king's position as the largest and ultimate landowner, the *primus inter pares* or greatest of the magnates of the land.

Yet in the changing political and social structure of the kingdom lies much of the answer to our problem. The castle stood above all for lordship, local power. 'You shall have the lordship, in castle and in tower,' declare the envoys of the 'Young King', offering the border counties to the King of Scotland, in Jordan Fantosme's poem of the rebellion of 1173–4. There can be no doubt that the steadily increasing royal power in the earlier Middle Ages resulted in an increasingly centralised state in which private fortresses became something of an anachronism, and hence, in consequence, the maintenance of royal castles throughout the realm became less necessary also. It is, again, a striking fact that 'between the Norman Conquest and the accession of Edward I (1272) there were only two periods when general peace was maintained in England for thirty consecutive years' (Professor Sir Frank Stenton). Certainly the remaining centuries of the Middle Ages did not witness the end of rebellion or civil war, but there was none the less an important change. From the thirteenth century onwards rebellion became less the result of personal grievance and more the expression of a wider political opposition. The undoubted personal grievances of the magnates who rose against King John in the last years of his reign were to some extent welded into the responsible programme of general reform embodied in Magna Carta: the baronial opposition to Henry III in the mid-thirteenth century was at first even more markedly united in the demand for specific reforms in the royal government. Again, the spread of political consciousness, and a little of political power, downwards to the middle classes, increasingly rendered the ambitions of individual nobles ineffective against the Crown without the support of general political disaffection. Nor to these slow and subtle changes, tending to the growth of political responsibility and stability within the realm, must we omit to add the less lasting effects of the Hundred Years War with France in the fourteenth and fifteenth centuries: a foreign war which united king and magnates against a common enemy, and directed the attentions of the baronage, and the martial energies of the more militant amongst them, beyond the frontiers of the kingdom. As the result of these and other causes, the more facile rebellions of the earlier Middle Ages, their extent seldom more than the uneasy alliance of self-interested magnates, were changed into something at once less frequent and more serious, approaching closer to the clash of opposed parties, divided by more fundamental differences, within the community of the realm. Rebellion, in short, attained in the later Middle Ages to the dignity of civil war.

Economic and social changes also were at work to render the castle obsolete. The growth of trade and industry swelled the ranks of the middle classes who did not live in castles. Thomas Paycocke, the clothier, has left us his house at Coggeshall in Essex, beautiful but in no way fortified, standing in a row by the street's side, and though not lacking in pride, lacking all the pomp and circumstance of the dwellings of the military aristocracy. Thomas Spring of Lavenham is chiefly remembered now for his contribution towards the magnificent East Anglian church of Lavenham, one amongst the many great 'wool churches' of that and other areas. Towns grew in size and prosperity, and to some extent the declining strength of the castle was offset by the increasing fortification of towns, for their importance made them, rather than the castle, the objective of the warfare of larger armies. Meanwhile the character of the ruling class itself changed gradually but decisively in the long course of the Middle Ages. The hard-fighting Norman kings and baronage, who had first raised castles in England, were transformed into a sophisticated aristocracy, owing allegiance to a sovereign more aloof in the mysteries of government and touched at times with divinity. And the knights who once followed their lords to war simply as soldiers proficient in the art of fighting on horseback, became a chivalrous order and a social class of gentry and local administrators, the forerunners of the country squires and Justices of the Peace.

The changing structure of the kingdom, and the changing standards of the upper classes especially, we have seen directly reflected in the architectural history of the castle, which, in the later Middle Ages, increasingly abandons serious fortification for a dignified comfort, or else is given over to decay. But it must be emphasised that these changes

196

were slow, and though the great age of the castle should probably be placed in the twelfth and thirteenth centuries, its importance in war and peace long continued, augmented no doubt by long-established outlook and habit—just as the traditions of a military aristocracy continued to demand a façade of martial splendour upon their new houses. Only perhaps by the mid-sixteenth century was the effective history of the castle as a combined fortress and residence, save for one brief exception later, at an end, as the unfortified Tudor country houses on the one hand, and Henry VIII's purely military coastal forts on the other, abundantly testify. Some half-century later a 'Certificate of His Majesties decayed Castells', amongst the State Papers and dated November 1609, makes depressing but instructive reading. Rochester, Guildford and Oxford of many others, Colchester, Norwich and Richmond, all are 'decayed', though some are still used for His Majesty's Justices of Assize on their Circuit. The great Edwardian Welsh castles of Conway, Beaumaris and Rhuddlan are 'Utterlie decayed'; Carnarvon is 'Utterlye decayed saving the Gatehouse which is in reasonable repaire and used for the countye prison'. Carew, an outstanding exception, is 'In good repaire', and Tickhill is listed as 'Used only for a dwelling house'.

Yet forty years later still, after over a century of more or less unbroken peace, the outbreak of the seventeenth-century Civil War, which knew no clear divisions of districts, classes or even families, caused ancient, long-neglected castles to be put once more into a state of defence. In the years which followed, many of them—and some hastily fortified and gallantly defended manor-houses as well—held out stoutly, usually for the King, sometimes in local conflicts and sometimes against the full force of Parliamentary armies. To the story of campaigns and the great battles of Naseby and Marston Moor which decided the issue of the war, we may add as footnotes, interesting yet unimportant, the sieges of Corfe and Colchester, Raglan and Pembroke, Donnington, Bolton, Newark and many more. It is impossible to regret this last curiously postponed hour of the castles' military glory, and impossible not to resent the ignoble fate which came to so many of them afterwards. For Cromwell and the Parliamentary leaders, determined that such local resistance should not be possible again, systematically demolished and 'slighted' those castles which they took, and reduced most of them at once to such ruin as even now, after three more centuries, time could not yet have achieved.

'And now it is all gone—like an unsubstantial pageant faded.' So wrote Froude, in a splendid passage of his *History,* on the passing of the Middle Ages. But there is nothing unsubstantial about the castle, even in its ruins, and, indeed, the Middle Ages are not gone. They live on in their institutions, Church, King, Parliament and University, which have survived them; in the great mass of learning, books and records they have left behind; and, most immediately of all perhaps, in the architecture they have bequeathed us. Of all the buildings of the Middle Ages none are more characteristic nor were more important in their time than the castles, which yet remain throughout the land, affording to those who care to seek it direct access to the past.

Appendix

'Licence to Crenellate' Allington Castle, Kent, 1281

[*Note: This licence, now at the Public Record Office (Ref. E 329/470), and reproduced in Figure 46, is in the form of Letters Patent. It runs in the name of the king, Edward I, and bears his Great Seal. The seal, in green wax suspended on silk cords, shows on the obverse (front) the king in majesty, and on the reverse (shown in our illustration) the king armed and mounted. A photograph of Allington Castle in its present condition appears as Figure 47.*]

TEXT

Edwardus Dei gratia rex Anglie, dominus Hibernie et dux Aquitannie, omnibus ad quos presentes littere pervenerint salutem. Sciatis quod concessimus pro nobis et heredibus nostris dilecto et fideli nostro Stephano de Penecestr' et Margarete uxori eius quod domum suam de Alinton' in comitatu Kancie muro de petra et calce firmare et kernellare, et eam sic firmatam et kernellatam tenere possint sibi et heredibus suis imperpetuum sine occasione vel impedimento nostri vel heredum nostrorum aut ministrorum quorumcunque. In cuius rei testimonium has litteras nostras fieri fecimus patentes. Teste me ipso apud Westmonasterium, vicesimo tercio die Maii anno regni nostri nono.

TRANSLATION

Edward by the grace of God King of England, Lord of Ireland and Duke of Aquitaine, to all to whom these letters come, greeting. Know that we have granted on behalf of ourselves and our heirs to our beloved and faithful Stephen of Penchester and Margaret his wife that they may fortify and crenellate their house at Allington in the county of Kent with a wall of stone and lime, and that they and their heirs may hold it, thus fortified and crenellated, for ever, without let or hindrance of us or our heirs or any of our officials. In witness whereof we have caused these our letters to be made patent. Witnessed by myself at Westminster on the twenty-third day of May in the ninth year of our reign.

Medieval Seal of Rochester

Index

The references in heavy type are to the figure-numbers
of the illustrations.

Place-names indicate castles unless otherwise stated

203

205

206

207